Latham, Frank Brown, 1910-.

The transcontinental railroad, 1862-69

DATE			

The driving of the Last Spike at Promontory Point, Utah, on May 10, 1869, signified the meeting of the rails of the Union Pacific and Central Pacific railroads — and the completion of the nation's first transcontinental road. The building of this line was the greatest engineering feat of its day and still deserves to rank among the great construction feats of all time.

The completion of the transcontinental, ahead of schedule, cut the travel time between California and the East to days instead of weeks. It linked the agriculture, industry, and commerce of the Pacific and Atlantic coasts and opened the Great Plains of the West to settlement. And it launched the great boom in railroad building, which saw the construction of three more transcontinental roads within the next twenty years.

In time the railroad age gave way to the automobile age. Then came the air age and the jet age. But the railroad age, particularly the building of the transcontinental, remains a great landmark in American history.

PRINCIPALS

THEODORE DEHONE JUDAH, who dreamed of a transcontinental railroad but did not live to see his dream come true.

PRESIDENT ABRAHAM LINCOLN, who saw the railroad as a great unifying influence during the Civil War.

THE "BIG FOUR," who took control of the Central Pacific:

LELAND STANFORD, president of the CP; COLLIS POTTER HUNTINGTON, vice-president; MARK HOPKINS, treasurer; CHARLES CROCKER, chief of construction, who assured success by hiring thousands of Chinese workers.

DR. THOMAS C. DURANT, vice-president and chief executive of the Union Pacific, who saw no hope of profit in the UP and said his idea was to "grab a wad of money" and get out.

SILAS SEYMOUR, the engineer hired by Dr. Durant to change the routes of the UP in order to collect more government loan bonds and land grants.

GRENVILLE MELLEN DODGE, chief engineer of the UP, who opposed the Durant-Seymour schemes.

GENERAL ULYSSES S. GRANT, who backed Dodge.

OAKES AMES, the wealthy shovel manufacturer who, at Lincoln's request, invested heavily in the UP and fought Dr. Durant for control of the railroad.

GENERAL JACK CASEMENT, Champion Track Layer of the Continent, who took the contract to lay UP rails from Omaha to Ogden, Utah.

MAJOR FRANK NORTH'S PAWNEE SCOUTS, who protected the UP workers.

SIOUX CHIEF RED CLOUD, who warned the UP surveyors: "We do not want you here. You are scaring away the buffalo."

GENERAL WILLIAM T. SHERMAN, who doubted the road could be built, then became a strong supporter of Dodge and the Union Pacific.

15
15
U. P. RY

The Transcontinental Railroad, 1862–69

A Great Engineering Feat Links America Coast to Coast

By Frank B. Latham

FRANKLIN WATTS, INC.
NEW YORK / 1973

Frontispiece: a Union Pacific construction crew and U.S. troops fight off an Indian attack (from a contemporary painting).

For Lucille and Linda

The authors and publishers of the Focus Books wish to acknowledge the helpful editorial suggestions of Professor Richard B. Morris

Photographs courtesy of:
Association of American Railroads: pages 12 (lower), 19, 38 (upper), 40, 42, 45 (upper and lower), 53, 56, 76; Charles Phelps Cushing: pages 12 (upper), 84; Union Pacific Railroad Museum Collection: pages ii, vi, 4, 11, 22, 27, 30, 33, 35 (upper and lower), 38 (lower), 49, 61, 62, 66, 73, 79, 80.

LIBRARY OF CONGRESS CATALOGING IN PUBLICATION DATA

Latham, Frank Brown, 1910–
The transcontinental railroad, 1862–69.

(A Focus book)
SUMMARY: Traces the conception, planning, and building of the first transcontinental railroad and discusses its effects on the lives of the American people.
Bibliography: p.
1. Union Pacific Railroad–Juvenile literature. 2. Central Pacific Railroad–Juvenile literature. [1. Union Pacific Railroad. 2. Central Pacific Railroad]
I. Title.
HE2791.U55L37 385'.0973 73-1222
ISBN 0-531-01025-2

Printed in the United States of America
6 5 4 3 2 1

Contents

A stagecoach of the Overland Trail. Such coaches were a common form of transportation across the United States before the transcontinental railroad was completed.

Introduction

The building of the transcontinental railroad was the greatest engineering feat of its day, comparable in our time to the landing of astronauts on the moon. And indeed, to many Americans of the early 1800's, the wilderness stretching for hundreds of miles west of the Missouri River seemed almost as inaccessible as the moon.

The Overland Trail, a natural thoroughfare used by Indians, fur trappers, and explorers, meandered 2,000 miles from the Missouri River to the Pacific coast. The northern branches of this great pathway — the Oregon Trail and the California Trail — were used increasingly in the 1840's by land-hungry settlers. Then the discovery of gold in California brought a rush of men to the goldfields. Some of the forty-niners traveled by sailing ship around Cape Horn (the southern tip of South America) to San Francisco — a trip that took from three to four months. Others sailed to Panama, traveled overland across the Isthmus, and then took a ship to San Francisco — a journey of some four to five weeks. But most of the forty-niners traveled overland in Conestoga wagons pulled by yokes of oxen at 2 miles an hour. They organized trains of twenty to thirty wagons for protection against hostile Indians. This trip took from four to six months and hundreds of people died on the way — the victims of Indians, disease, desert heat, or blizzards.

In 1861 the establishment of the Overland Stage Line by Ben Holladay, which used 100 Concord coaches and 2,700 horses and mules, was hailed as a great step forward in transportation. The 1,900-mile journey on the Overland Stage took seventeen days at full speed, cost the passenger $225, and safe arrival was none too certain.

The demand for speed in carrying mail was answered by the Pony Express in 1860. Its riders delivered letters on tissue paper for $1 a half-ounce from St. Joseph, Missouri, to Placerville, California, in eight days. Carrying only a mail pouch, a bowie knife, and a revolver, each rider traveled 250 miles a day. Then, in 1861, the Overland Telegraph put the Pony Express riders out of business.

Despite the progress that had been made, far-seeing men had for years argued that a railroad was needed to provide quick and dependable transportation between the East and the Pacific coast. They were dismissed as impractical dreamers by critics who were fond of quoting Senator Daniel Webster's speech in the Senate: "What do we want of that vast and worthless area? That region of savages and wild beasts, of deserts, of shifting sands and swirling winds, of dust, of cactus, of prairie dogs. To what use could we even put these endless mountain ranges? What could we do with the Western coast of three thousand miles, rockbound and cheerless and uninviting?" In another speech, Webster thanked God that "the Great Stony Mountains [the Rockies] would ever be an impenetrable barrier between the East and California!" When plans for a railroad finally were given serious consideration, rivalry between the North and South, whose leaders could not agree on the route such a road might follow, stalled it in Congress.

During the Civil War (1861–65), the proposed transcontinental road won the support of men who looked upon it as a military necessity — a link between the East and gold-rich California and the other territories and states of the Far West. Congress passed the Pacific Railroad Bill in 1862, and the dreamers and builders went to work. When one considers the scanty equipment at hand and the obstacles faced by the men who conquered heat, deserts, blizzards, and mountains, the building of the transcontinental still deserves to rank among the great engineering feats of all time.

The Union Pacific, building west out of Omaha, Nebraska, and the Central Pacific, building east out of Sacramento, California, laid 1,776 miles of rails without the aid of bulldozers, steam shovels, pneumatic drills, or computers. The transcontinental was a "handmade" road: grading crews with plows, scrapers, picks, and shovels leveled the roadbed and dropped ties, 5 to the rail length; then 10 "ironmen," 5 to each 700-pound rail (the Central Pacific rail weighed 500 pounds), pulled the iron from a wagon and dropped it onto the ties; spikers and clampers swiftly fastened it into place — 30 seconds to each pair of rails, 2 rail lengths to the minute, 3 blows to each spike, 10 spikes to the rail, 400 rails and 4,000 spikes and 12,000 blows to the mile. Seldom was less than a mile of track laid in a day, and often 3, 4, 5, or more miles were laid. Every mile of track took more than 2,500 ties, delivered by 6- and 8-horse or mule teams. In the towering, seemingly unconquerable Sierra Nevada mountains, the Central Pacific's patient, tireless Chinese coolies chipped their way through granite at the rate of 7 inches a day, then used gunpowder and later nitroglycerine to blast out fifteen tunnels.

Although the Union Pacific was building from the East, it had no eastern rail connection between Omaha and Chicago until 1867. Thus rails, ties, food, and all other supplies had to be shipped up the Missouri River from St. Louis or hauled 100 miles by wagon across Iowa from the nearest railhead. Then supplies had to be ferried across the unbridged Missouri from Council Bluffs, Iowa, to Omaha and loaded onto railroad cars for the trip west. All the way to the Black Hills, 500 miles from the Missouri, there was little timber for ties, except for inferior cottonwood. Oak ties, obtained as far east as Pennsylvania and New York, cost $3.50

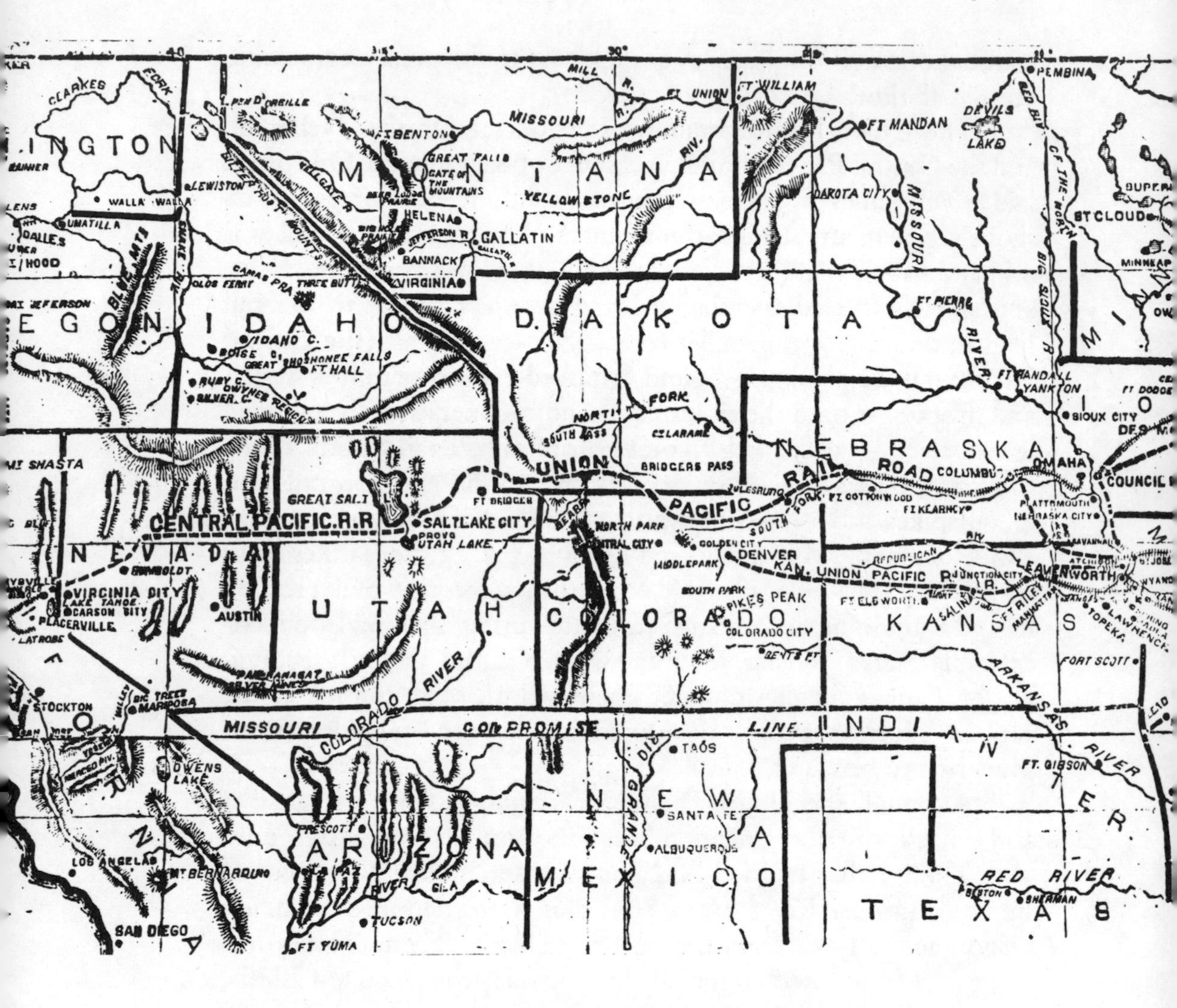

A map published in the New York Daily Tribune *in 1867, showing the routes of the Central Pacific and Union Pacific. The two lines met in May, 1869 at Promontory Point, Utah, just north of Salt Lake City.*

each delivered at Omaha. Beyond Omaha for around 1,000 miles, there were no settlements of any size, no industries, no farm produce except for skimpy supplies of hay cut by a few ranchers and usually purchased by the Army and freighting outfits. Grain cost $7 a bushel and hay went for $34 a ton. Most supplies had to be brought from Omaha on a single-track railroad through a country swarming with Indians who were desperately fighting to protect their hunting grounds from the white invaders and their "iron horse."

The Central Pacific had an even more difficult supply problem. Except for ties and timbers, California produced little that was needed by the railroad. Rails, locomotives, and other equipment had to be shipped at great cost around Cape Horn or across Panama and then by ship to San Francisco. Rails cost an average of $91.70 at the mills in the East; freight rates averaged $17.50 a ton by the "Horn," and over $50.00 a ton by Panama. The CP always had at least $1,000,000 worth of material in shipment by the hazardous water route. Delays were frequent owing to storms or wrecks, and during the war emergency, the Union government might suddenly take over a load of material bound for the Central Pacific.

When the transcontinental was completed — ahead of schedule — it cut travel time between California and the East to days instead of weeks. It linked the agriculture, industry, and commerce of the Pacific and Atlantic coasts and opened the Great Plains of the West to settlement. It also launched the great boom in railroad construction, which saw the building of the Southern Pacific Railroad; the Atchison, Topeka and Sante Fe; the Northern Pacific; and many other railroads.

Men and an Idea

In 1832 a man of vision whose name remains unknown wrote an article for a weekly newspaper, the *Emigrant*, published in Ann Arbor, Michigan. He suggested a plan for a railroad to run from New York City by way of the Great Lakes and the Platte River to Oregon. At that time, there were only 140 miles of railroad track in the United States, and the puny locomotives then in use could never have climbed the mountains of the Far West. So no one took this idea seriously — except several other visionaries. Also in 1832, Dr. Hartwell Carver of Rochester, New York, proposed to Congress that a railroad, resting on stone foundations, be built from New York to San Francisco Bay. In 1838, the Reverend Samuel Parker, a pioneer missionary on the Oregon Trail, insisted that a railroad to the Pacific was practicable. Lilburn W. Boggs, a former governor of Missouri, drew up a plan for a transcontinental railroad in 1843. The next year, Senator Thomas H. Benton of Missouri, father-in-law of Western explorer John Charles Frémont, predicted that "Asiatic commerce" would in the not-too-distant future cross the mountains by rail from San Francisco.

In 1845 Senator John M. Niles of Connecticut presented to Congress a plan drawn up by Asa Whitney, a New York merchant and Oriental traveler. He wanted the government to set aside for a railroad 75,000,000 acres of land in a strip 60 miles wide from the Mississippi to the Columbia River. Whitney said the building of the railroad could be financed by land sales, mining, lumbering, and industrial development. He further pointed out that the road would tie the northern states to the Far West and also be the cheapest and quickest means of handling ocean trade between the Far East and Europe. Instead of sending goods by the long route around South America or Africa, shippers could send goods to San Francisco, then by rail to New York for shipment to Europe.

Southern members of Congress blocked Whitney's proposal. They wanted a southern route by way of El Paso, Texas, to San Diego, California. In 1853 James Gadsden of South Carolina, who supported the southern route, became U.S. minister to Mexico. He engineered a deal by which the government bought a strip of desert land stretching from the Rio Grande River to California. This so-called Gadsden Purchase would be part of the right-of-way for a proposed Deep South railroad to the Pacific. At this time Secretary of War Jefferson Davis of Mississippi got Congress to approve a plan to send out survey parties to investigate routes for a transcontinental railroad. When the survey reports came to him in 1854, Davis decided — to no one's surprise — that the Gadsden route was the shortest, cheapest, and most practical. However, Northern leaders in Congress turned down the Gadsden route, and Southerners, already embittered by the North's growing opposition to the extension of slavery in the territories, refused to consider any other rail route.

Even so, pressure for a transcontinental (Pacific) railroad was building up in the country. The Mormons (Latter-day Saints), who had left Illinois to escape persecution and then turned parts of arid Utah into a garden spot under the leadership of Brigham Young, supported California in petitioning Congress for a railroad connection to the East. Rails were stretching across Iowa, toward the Missouri River, and railroad promoters were looking to the Great Plains and beyond.

The Mississippi and Missouri Railroad, which was building in Iowa, dispatched a young engineer, Grenville Mellen Dodge, to determine the best point for a railroad to touch the Missouri River. A native of Danvers, Massachusetts, born in 1831, and a graduate of the Norwich, Vermont, Military and Scientific Academy, Dodge had gone west in 1852 and gotten a job as a surveyor with Peter M. Dey of the Mississippi and Missouri. As Dey's chief assistant, Dodge was in charge of the survey from Davenport to Iowa City. From that town, he pushed westward and reached the Missouri River near Council Bluffs, Iowa, on November 22, 1853. Here he was to make his permanent home. In 1854, he married Anne Brown, a Peru, Illinois, girl he had met when he first came west. For several years, Dodge was busy on railroad construction and also ran a store in Council Bluffs as well as a freighting company. He later made surveys in the Platte River Valley of Nebraska Territory for Henry Farnam and Dr. Thomas C. Durant of the Chicago & Rock Island Railway.

Dr. Durant, who was born in Hinsdale, Massachusetts, in 1820, graduated with honors from Albany Medical College in 1840 and took a post as assistant professor. He left Albany in 1844 and joined an uncle who was trading on the New York Grain Exchange. Dr. Durant became a specialist in the movement of wheat down the Great Lakes and through the Erie Canal to the East. This led him into promoting the building of railroads in the Midwest.

Two years after Dodge had started surveying in the West, 27-year-old Theodore Dehone Judah went to California to build a 22-mile railroad between Sacramento and Folsom, California. Judah was born on March 4, 1826, in Bridgeport, Connecticut, and then moved with his family to Troy, New York, when his father, the Reverend Henry R. Judah, became pastor of Saint Paul's. Young Judah studied engineering at Rensselaer Polytechnic Institute in 1838–39 and soon became a promising railroad engineer. While working on a road in Connecticut, Judah met Anna, the daughter of John J. Pierce of Greenfield, a prominent and wealthy New Englander. Theodore and Anna were married in 1847 and moved to New York, where Judah served as location engineer for the Niagara Gorge and Erie Railroad.

When Judah moved to California to work on the Sacramento and Folsom line, he already had a dream of a transcontinental railroad. His wife Anna recalled his saying: "It will be built, and I'm going to have something to do with it." When the Sacramento-Folsom road was done, Judah took other surveying jobs and started exploring the Sierra Nevada range, with an eye toward a route to the East. He was so persistent in discussing his railroad ideas that people began to call him "crazy Judah." But he kept at it and helped to organize the Pacific Railroad Convention that met in San Francisco in September, 1859. Delegates from Washington Territory, Oregon, and California informed Congress that California was ready to build a railroad to the state line to meet another road building from the East. Judah then was sent to Washington to interest Congress in a transcontinental railroad. But the bitter struggle over slavery sidetracked all talk of railroad building. A man of great honesty and integrity, Judah submitted an expense account of only $40 for his Washington trip.

That same year, 1859, a rising Republican politician, Abraham Lincoln, came to Council Bluffs. Dodge was introduced to him as the man who knew more about railroads than anyone in that part of the country. Lincoln quickly maneuvered Dodge to a bench on the porch of the Pacific House.

"Dodge," he said, "what's the best route for a Pacific railroad?"

"From this town out the Platte Valley," was Dodge's instant response. For many minutes, Lincoln closely questioned the young engineer. Then the two men walked to a tall hill and looked west into the hazy vastness of the Great Plains. Between them and the Pacific Coast there was not a mile of rail line, except for the 22-mile stretch Theodore Judah had built in the Sacramento Valley.

A year later, Dodge and Henry Farnam were among Lincoln's Iowa supporters when he won the Republican nomination for President at the convention in Chicago. Another Iowa man, John A. Kasson of Des Moines, helped to write the Republican party platform of promises to the voters. Among these promises was a strong statement favoring the building — with government aid — of a Pacific (transcontinental) railroad.

Dodge attended Lincoln's inauguration and wrote his wife: "Old Abe delivered the greatest speech of the age. It is backbone all over." Six Southern states already had left the Union, and in his letter Dodge commented on the tension in Washington: "The city bristles with bayonets." In another letter to his wife, Dodge wrote of "our crowd," meaning Farnam, Dr. Durant, and others interested in a Pacific railroad, and added: "We are busy before the railroad committees."

Back in California, Judah spent the final months of 1860 prowling the Sierra Nevada, still seeking the best route for his dream railroad. One day he came upon the Emigrant and Donner passes, through which an old wagon road crossed the Sierras. Donner Pass and the nearby lake got their names from the "Donner Party," a wagon train that had become snowbound in that area in 1846-47 and lost many of its members through starvation. Although the Emigrant Pass–Donner Pass route was too steep for locomotives, and thus would require many tunnels, Judah concluded that it was the best way through the Sierras. He hurried back to the drugstore of his friend, Dr. Daniel Strong, in the mining camp of Dutch Flat. There, Judah wrote "The Articles of Association of the Central Pacific Railroad of Cali-

The meeting between General Grenville M. Dodge and Abraham Lincoln at Council Bluffs in 1859.

fornia." Leaving Dr. Stone to sell shares of stock to local residents, Judah sought the financial aid of prominent Californians.

At a meeting in Sacramento, he found four men who were later to take over the building of the Central Pacific. They were all easterners (three New Yorkers and a Connecticut Yankee) who had moved to California during and after the gold-rush days. Leland Stanford, born in Watervliet, New York, in 1824, had become a lawyer in New York and Wisconsin and then traveled by wagon train to California, where he soon prospered in the grocery business. He was to win election as Republican governor of California. Later, he established Leland Stanford, Jr., University as a memorial to his son. Charles Crocker, born in Troy, New York, in 1822, had moved with his family to an Indiana farm and then left home with "a shirt and a pair of socks wrapped in a handkerchief" to make his own way. He joined a wagon train that reached California in 1850 and tried mining, then opened the leading dry goods store in Sacramento. Collis Potter Huntington and Mark Hopkins were partners in the firm of Huntington and Hopkins, dealers in hardware and miners' supplies, in Sacramento. Huntington, born in Harwinton, Connecticut, in 1821, went to Oneonta, New York, to clerk in a store owned by his brother. Hearing later of "gold for the picking up in California," he headed for San Francisco by the Panama route. Mark Hopkins, born in Henderson, New York, in 1813, studied law as a training for business, moved west to Michigan and then on to California by land.

After several meetings in the Huntington and Hopkins store,

Above: A portrait of Leland Stanford, one of the founders of the Central Pacific Railroad and its first president. Below: Collis P. Huntington, a founder of the Central Pacific railroad and its first vice president.

the Central Pacific Railroad Company of California was organized on June 28, 1861. Stanford was chosen president; Huntington, vice-president; Hopkins, treasurer; James Bailey, a friend of Judah's, secretary; Charles Crocker, chief of construction. Crocker's brother, Edwin, was one of the company directors. Judah was selected chief engineer, and he later hired Samuel S. Montague as assistant engineer. Montague had worked for Peter Dey and served on engineering parties with Dodge for a year. Lured to Denver, Colorado, by the Pikes Peak gold rush, Montague joined a wagon train bound for California in 1860. He was an engineer for the Sacramento Valley Railroad when Judah hired him.

When Judah completed his survey for the Central Pacific in mid-September, the directors of the company ordered him to go to Washington to obtain land grants and bonds from the government to aid in building the road. Soon Vice-President Huntington followed Judah to Washington to win friends for the Central Pacific.

Congress Finally Acts

In Washington, the "Little Congress" — so-called because the Southern members had gone south to join the new Confederate States of America — was too harried by war problems to give attention to railroad legislation. But in January, 1862, Representative Aaron Sargent of California, armed with notes from Judah, introduced another Pacific Railroad Bill in the House. Scoffed Representative Owen Lovejoy of Illinois: "Do I understand the gentleman of California to say that he actually expects this road to be built?"

Sargent replied: "The gentleman of Illinois may understand me to predict that if this bill is passed the road will be finished within ten years." The bill, as amended by the Senate and House committees, soon picked up strong support. Members of Congress saw that the railroad would help keep the state of California and the Nevada Territory loyal to the Union at a time when the armies of the Confederacy appeared to be winning the war. The bill passed the Senate on June 20, 1862, and the House on June 24. It was signed by President Lincoln on July 1, 1862. It was just one of several important acts approved by Congress and the President in 1862 to strengthen the Union. The Morrill Act provided federal land grants to each state and territory for the founding of a college of agriculture and mechanics. The many great state universities of today grew from this act. The Homestead Act offered 160 acres of land in the West to any citizen who would live on it for five years. A third act created an independent Department of Agriculture under a commissioner.

The title of the Pacific Railroad Act read: "An act to aid in the construction of a railroad and telegraph line from the Missouri River to the Pacific Coast, and to secure to the Government the use of the same for postal, military and other purposes." To accommodate other state-chartered railroads that wanted to connect with the transcontinental, the act specified that the new Union Pacific Railroad "shall commence at a point on the one hundredth meridian" (which crosses Nebraska some 60 miles west of present-day Kearney). The Leavenworth, Pawnee and Western Railroad, a Kansas company, was authorized to build north to the 100th meridian; so was the Hannibal and St. Joseph. The Union Pacific Railroad, which was to build westward to meet the Central Pacific at the California-Nevada border, was also to build eastward from the 100th meridian to a point — to be picked by the President of the United States — on the western border of Iowa. The Leavenworth, Pawnee and Western never did build north to meet the Union Pacific in Nebraska. By an act of Congress in 1866, it was permitted to change its route. The L. P. and W. became the Kansas Pacific and laid track up the Smoky Hill River Valley of Kansas, finally reaching Denver, Colorado.

The above-named roads, particularly the Union Pacific and the Central Pacific, were granted "vacant" lands within 10 miles on either side of their tracks for five alternate sections per mile. (The Indians did not consider any of this land "vacant," and were ready to fight for it.) As further financial aid, the government would lend bonds, payable in 30 years at 6 percent interest, at the following rate: on mountain construction, $48,000 per mile of track; on construction to the base of mountains, $16,000 per mile; on construction across the high desert between the Rockies and the Sierras, $32,000 per mile. The whole amount of the government loan was not to exceed $50,000,000. Government commissioners should inspect each 40 miles of railroad and telegraph line. Upon the commissioners' approval of the work, the bonds and the land grants should be issued.

The act further provided that if the Union Pacific should

reach the California border before the Central Pacific, it might continue on, with the consent of the state, to another meeting point. And if the CP arrived first, it, too, might keep on building. The CP was to complete 50 miles of road within the first two years of agreeing to the act, and 50 miles each year following. The UP was to complete 100 miles of road and telegraph line west of the Iowa border within the first two years, and 100 miles a year thereafter. The connection at the California-Nevada border should be made within twelve years, or before July 1, 1874, and there must be "a continuous line of railroad, ready for use, from the Missouri River to the navigable waters of the Sacramento River, in California, by the first day of July, eighteen hundred and seventy-six."

Judah studied the Pacific Railroad Act and wired President Stanford of the Central Pacific: "We have drawn the elephant. Now let us see if we can harness him up." There were those who remained unconvinced, however. General William T. Sherman wrote his brother, Senator John Sherman of Ohio: "A railroad to the Pacific? I would hate to buy a ticket on it for my grandchildren!" One of the strong believers in the road, who later made a believer out of General Sherman, was Grenville M. Dodge. When war came, he had immediately volunteered and, as colonel of the Fourth Iowa Infantry, was wounded at the Battle of Pea Ridge in 1862. He then was sent to the staff of General Henry Halleck and ordered to untangle the wreckage along the Gulf & Mobile Railroad, created by Confederates retreating after the Battle of Shiloh. News of the passage of the Pacific Railroad Act made Dodge impatient to get back to peacetime railroad engineering.

The Central Pacific

Ground-breaking ceremonies for the Central Pacific took place in Sacramento on January 8, 1863. Leland Stanford, who had been governor of California for almost a year, turned the first spadeful of dirt. The construction firm of Charles Crocker & Co. already had been given the contract for the grading, masonry, bridges, and track for 18 miles of road out of Sacramento. But sales of stock in the Central Pacific had been slow; San Francisco citizens, jealous of Sacramento, bought only ten shares in one day. The CP had only about $156,000 on hand, and Chief Engineer Judah estimated that the first 50 miles of track would cost over $3,000,000 — or $68,000 a mile. Moreover, 40 miles of track had to be completed before the CP could obtain government bonds and land grants. Turned down by San Francisco bankers, Huntington spent most of his time in the East trying to raise money. Wartime conditions naturally made investors cautious and money scarce.

Companies that saw their business threatened by the Central Pacific going through were busy attacking the road with whispering campaigns. "The road," they said, "will end high in the air and no where else." For example, the Wells Fargo Express Company, which controlled the main traffic between California and Nevada, was disturbed by the thought of CP competition. The Overland Stage Company, running cross-country from Missouri to California, felt it would be doomed by a transcontinental road. The Pacific Mail Steamship Company, which handled the traffic across Panama and up the coast to San Francisco, naturally opposed a transcontinental line.

Friends of Huntington and Stanford warned them: "You will bury your fortunes in the Sierras." It was true that the per-

The California Terminus of the Central Pacific Railroad at Oakland. Here, ocean-going freight could be transferred directly to rails. Note train approaching at right.

sonal fortunes of Huntington, Stanford, Crocker, and Hopkins had been pledged to obtain shipments of rails from Pennsylvania manufacturers. Even so, these men took steps to protect themselves. Governor Stanford did not hesitate to use his political power to obtain favors from the California legislature. During 1863 and 1864, the legislature passed acts authorizing the state and several counties to issue bonds to be used for the purchase of 165,000 shares of CP stock.

The CP itself was allowed to issue $12,000,000 worth of bonds, and the interest on these bonds was to be paid by the state treasury, *not* the railroad. This use of public (state) money for private profit upset the honest Ted Judah. He was appalled when the "Big Four"—Stanford, Huntington, Hopkins, and Crocker—organized The Associates (later called the Construction & Finance Company) to take over construction of the CP. This meant that the Big Four, which controlled the CP, would hire themselves (The Associates) to build the railroad and make a big profit by overcharging themselves. The losers in this deal were the U.S. government and the state, some counties, and private investors who put money into the CP.

Then Huntington came up with yet another idea. The Pacific Railroad Act provided for loans from the government of $48,000 a mile for track laid in the mountains, but only $16,000 per mile for track laid up to the base of the mountains. With this in mind, Huntington asked J. W. Whitney, the state geologist, an important question: "Where does the base of the Sierra Nevada begin?" Whitney said the base began where the brown earth of the Sacramento Valley met the red soil of the Sierras. Huntington chortled. If the Department of the Interior scientists in Washington and President Lincoln accepted Whitney's report, the Central Pacific could get government loans of $48,000 for building track across gently rolling terrain. Engineer Judah violently objected to "moving" the Sierras 24 miles nearer Sacramento. The Big Four ignored Judah and sent Whitney's report to Washington. The Department of the Interior scientists agreed, and Abraham Lincoln, harried by war problems, accepted their word without question and signed an order moving the base of the Sierras. "Here is a case," commented the shrewd Charles Crocker, "where Abraham's faith has moved mountains." This action brought the CP an additional $480,000 in government loans, and it enabled Huntington to borrow money from previously tight-fisted bankers in New York and Boston.

Again Judah protested angrily at the policies of the Big Four. They countered by offering to buy out his interest in the CP for $100,000; or Judah could buy out the Big Four if he could raise the money. Bitterly disappointed that his "dream railroad" had fallen into the hands of scheming, selfish men, Judah boarded a ship for New York. He hoped to find investors who would buy control of the road for him. He caught yellow fever during the trip and died a week after he reached New York, on November 2, 1863. The Big Four passed a resolution of sympathy to Anna Judah and got on with the business of building a road that had been made possible by the genius and persistence of Theodore D. Judah.

Samuel C. Montague replaced Judah as chief engineer of the CP. J. H. Strobridge became superintendent of construction under Charles Crocker, who had the contract for the first 18 miles of road. These 18 miles presented the engineers with many problems. Hydraulic mining up the American River washed tons of dirt and rocks (called tailings) into the stream, causing it to flood. A heavy fill had to be built to lift the railroad grade for 3 miles over the flooded lands. The piles supporting the bridge across the American River had to be driven through 15 to 20 feet of tailings.

Work began in February, 1863, and was not completed to

Junction (present-day Rossville) until the early winter of that year. At Junction, the CP announced plans to build on to Newcastle, 31 miles from Sacramento. Crocker bid for these 13 miles, but because of complaints that he was the favorite of the CP, he was given only 2 miles. The other 11 miles were apportioned among several contractors.

Soon there was trouble as the contractors bid against each other for scarce labor and wages went up rapidly. There were also strikes that delayed the work, and finally the bulk of the 13 miles of grading and track laying was turned over to Crocker. Newcastle was finally reached in July, 1864, a time of discouragement for the CP. The county bonds that had been wangled by Stanford to be used to purchase CP stock were delayed by foes of the CP. General Grant's army was bogged down in Virginia and war weariness swept the country. The value of the paper dollar dropped to 35 cents, and the CP treasury was about empty.

At this moment, the CP received a most welcome gift from the government. In July, 1864, Congress approved the Pacific Railroad Act of 1864, which amended the act of 1862. It helped assure the future of the Central Pacific and the Union Pacific. This new act doubled the land grants to ten sections per mile within 20 miles on either side of the tracks. Furthermore, it gave the railroads ownership of all minerals — coal, iron, copper — in the land grants. The government loan bonds were to be issued on the completion of each 20 miles of track in mountain areas, rather than 40 miles as provided in the 1862 act. Of much more importance to the railroads was a provision that permitted them to sell their own bonds in amounts equal to the government loan bonds.

Finally, the railroad bonds became first mortgages and the

Charles Crocker, the Central Pacific's Superintendent of Construction.

government bonds were reduced to second-mortgage rank. Under the 1862 act, government bonds were first mortgages, meaning that the railroads had to pay them off before they paid the holders of the railroad's second-mortgage bonds. In arguing for a change in the 1862 act, Huntington of the CP said that investors were reluctant to buy second-mortgage railroad bonds at a time when many men doubted that the CP and UP could ever be profitable even if they were finally built. Anxious to get the transcontinental road built and to protect the CP and UP against failure, Congress and President Lincoln agreed to all the changes suggested by the railroads.

The Union Pacific

Unlike the Central Pacific, which was a state-chartered road receiving federal government aid, the Union Pacific was created by Congress, and officials representing the U.S. government sat on its board of directors. In October, 1863, the Union Pacific Company was organized in New York City with thirty directors and the following officers: General John A. Dix, president; Dr. Thomas C. Durant, vice-president; Henry V. Poor, secretary; John J. Cisco, treasurer. General Dix took no active part in managing the road. These duties fell to Dr. Durant, who was chief executive, principal stockholder, business manager, and money raiser.

Investors were slow in coming forward with money to get the UP started. Again, doubts were expressed that the UP ever would make any money. Unlike the CP, which had to build only 50 miles to tap the traffic of the California and Nevada gold and silver mines, the UP had to build 1,500 miles of track into a wilderness containing few settlements. The whole Territory of Nebraska contained only around 35,000 people, and the country from central Nebraska to the Salt Lake Valley in Utah was looked upon as a barren waste.

While Dr. Durant was hunting for money in New York, General Dodge was called to Washington by President Lincoln. When Dodge entered the White House early in the spring of 1863, the President got right down to business. "Dodge," he said, "I want you to help me decide the commencement point of the Union Pacific Railroad." Lincoln explained that chief engineer Peter A. Dey had been put in charge of surveys, but he could not start work until a point had been selected for the UP terminus on the Missouri River. Kansas City and other towns were contending for this honor and the wily Dr. Durant had encouraged them in order to sell stock in the Union Pacific.

Lincoln and Dodge spread out maps and discussed various starting points. Then, on November 17, 1863, the President issued a proclamation fixing a township line "within the city of Omaha" (opposite Council Bluffs, Iowa) as the terminus of the Union Pacific. During their spring meeting the President and Dodge discussed the money problems of the Union Pacific. Dodge told Lincoln that second-mortgage railroad bonds were hard to sell to investors and that the government might have to take over the building of the railroad. Lincoln said the government was too burdened by the war to take over construction, but he promised Dodge that it would make any changes in the Pacific Railroad Act of 1862 that were needed to obtain more aid from private investors. Dodge reported this conversation to Dr. Durant, who later joined Huntington of the Central Pacific in urging the passage of the Pacific Railroad Act of 1864.

Ground-breaking ceremonies for the UP were held at Omaha on December 2, 1863, but actual construction was delayed almost a year to await financial backing. Forty miles of track had to be laid — at an estimated cost of $1,000,000 — before any government aid could be obtained, and private investors continued to shy away from UP stock. Meanwhile, the CP, with private and state aid, had started building from its Sacramento terminal. In the year and a half since the passage of the 1862 act, the UP had not built a foot of grade and time was running out. Then, on July 2, President Lincoln signed the act of 1864, which helped solve the financial problems of both the UP and the CP.

Following the example of the Big Four of the CP, Dr. Durant had set up a company called Credit Mobilier whose job was similar to that of the CP's Construction & Finance outfit. Credit Mobilier, owned by Durant and his friends, would build

A portrait of Thomas C. Durant, vice president and chief executive of the Union Pacific Railroad.

the railroad and overcharge the UP for its services. Thus, in August, 1864, Durant gave a contract to a crony, Hubert M. Hoxie, for the construction of the first 100 miles of road west of Omaha. Hoxie then turned this contract over to the Credit Mobilier at $50,000 a mile. Chief Engineer Peter Dey's per-mile cost had been set at $30,000, so the Credit Mobilier made about $20,000 a mile after giving Hoxie $10,000 worth of UP stock for his cooperation. This deal outraged Dey, who sent a bluntly worded resignation to Durant: "I do not," said Dey, "approve of the contract for building of the first hundred miles from Omaha west, and I do not care to have my name so connected with the railroad that I shall appear to endorse the contract." Later, he wrote his friend Dodge: "I am giving up the best position this country has ever offered any man."

Durant now offered Dodge the job of chief engineer. Dodge knew of Durant's reputation for slippery business deals, but he did not want to turn down such a challenging job. Dodge accepted the position but he also warned Durant that he would not stand for any meddling by him. "I will become chief engineer," said Dodge, "on condition that I be given absolute control in the field. You are about to build a railroad through a country that has neither law nor order, and whoever heads the work must be backed up. There must be no divided interests."

Durant was annoyed by Dodge's bluntness, but he needed a man who could direct thousands of tough workers, fight Indians, and lay a lot of track in a hurry; and he was sure that Dodge's past experience suited him for the task. After his talk with Lincoln in the spring of 1863, Dodge had returned to his Army duties. In 1864, he served both as a commander of combat forces and of railroad engineers under General William T. Sherman. During Sherman's advance on Atlanta, Georgia, Dodge's engineers built a bridge 14 feet high and 710 feet long over the Chattahoochee

River in three days. Sherman later swore that Dodge's men could build bridges and repair railroads as fast as his infantry could march.

The Civil War was the first major conflict in which railroads played an important part, and Dodge's work won him the rank of major general of volunteers and the commendation of General U. S. Grant, commander in chief of the Union armies. In the final months of the war, General Dodge was commander of the Military Department of Missouri and was then sent to command troops against the Indians in the West. During a scouting trip, Dodge and a small detachment of cavalry were attacked and, while escaping, discovered a pass through the Black Hills in what is now Wyoming. Dodge's interest in the Pacific railroad had not flagged, and he was aware than Union Pacific surveyors had been searching for a crossing of the Black Hills. So he marked the pass by a lone tree standing gaunt against the sky.

One of Dodge's first acts as chief engineer was to order James Evans to find Lone Tree Pass, as it was named, and run a survey in the Black Hills. Next, Dodge studied the problem of keeping supplies moving to workers as they built a railroad through a wilderness. It was solved when Dr. Durant gave the construction contract on the UP to the Champion Track Layer of the Continent — General John S. ("Jack") Casement — and his brother Dan. Jack Casement had commanded Ohio troops during the Civil War while his brother stayed home to run their construction business. The Casements and Dodge hit it off well, and Dodge quickly approved their plan to handle the supply problem.

The Casements devised a construction train that functioned like an assembly line on wheels. The leading unit of this train was a rail-laden flatcar that fed rails to the track layers. Behind the flatcar were the other units: a feed store and saddler's shop; a carpenter's shop and washhouse; two sleeping cars each 80 feet

General "Jack" Casement's construction train is shown here at "end o' track" in Wyoming. Casement is the figure standing in the foreground.

long, containing bunks for 144 men; two dining cars, each seating 200 men; a combined kitchen and telegrapher's car; a general store; seven more sleeping cars; a supply car and office; and two water cars.

Another unit that occasionally joined the Casement train was the Lincoln Car. Built for the President in 1864, it was ironclad and bulletproof. However, Lincoln, who was assassinated the following year, never used the car. On its first official trip it carried his body to Springfield, Illinois, for burial. Dr. Durant later bought this car from the government and it was used by guests, directors of the UP, and frequently by Dodge.

The majority of Casement's workers were ex-Confederate and ex-Union soldiers. There were men from Georgia and North and South Carolina; Swedes, Germans, and Danes from Chicago; and hundreds of Irish from the East, plus 300 or more Negroes. In case of an Indian attack, Casement's train could arm hundreds of men commanded by ex-army officers.

As the rails pushed westward, towns sprang up at the supply points from which "end 'o track" was supplied with rails, ties, food, and other equipment. Into these towns, which were called "Hell on Wheels," crowded merchants, peddlers, gamblers, saloonkeepers, dance-hall girls, thieves, gunmen, and assorted cutthroats, all eager to help the railroad workers get rid of their pay.

By the end of 1865, the UP had laid only 45 miles of track, and it needed to lay 202 miles in 11 months or else it would lose its government grants. With Dodge as chief engineer, the bearded, soft-spoken Samuel Reed as chief of construction, and Jack Casement directing his construction trains, the Union Pacific buckled down to work in 1866. Casement's ironmen charged up the Platte River Valley, laying a mile or more of track each day and fighting heat, storms, and Indians all the way. Red Cloud, chief of the Sioux, had personally warned the UP's surveyors to turn back or run the risk of losing their scalps. "We do not want you here," said Red Cloud. "You are scaring away the buffalo." As the UP advanced west, its meat hunters killed hundreds of buffalo, seriously cutting into the Indians' food supply.

The Central Pacific had no Indian problem. The Mexicans and the forty-niners had crushed Indian resistance in central California, and the Paiute War of 1861–62 had scattered Nevada's Indian tribes. Charles Crocker explained that he kept the Indians quiet and happy by giving the chiefs passes to ride the day coaches and letting the Indian braves hitch rides on the freight cars.

But the Union Pacific was building into the heart of the hunting grounds of the proud Sioux and Cheyenne — who were ready to fight to the death to halt the railroad. Reported General Dodge: "In making the surveys, numbers of our men, some of them the ablest and most promising, were killed; and during the construction, our stock was run off by the hundreds, I might say by the thousands; our cars and stations and ranches burned. Graders and track layers, tie cutters and station builders had to sleep under guard, and have gone to their work with their picks and shovels and their mechanical tools in one hand and their rifles in the other, and they often had to drop one and use the other."

Nevertheless, the men of the UP advanced despite all opposition. Several hundred miles ahead were the surveyors, seeking the best route for the road. Behind them were the graders with plows, scrapers, picks, and shovels. They were around 100 miles ahead of the track layers, and between them were gangs of bridge builders and tunnel workers. And up and down the line raged Jack Casement, his red beard bristling and his voice snapping and

A typical "hell on wheels" town along the Union Pacific some 950 miles west of Omaha. The town vanished within a few months after the track crew had moved on.

snarling as he urged his men to greater efforts. Back in Omaha and Council Bluffs, supplies were piled toward the sky as Dan Casement sent scores of trains west each day to brother Jack's workers. Every mile of track laid required 40 carloads of supplies — rails, ties, and other equipment, plus food.

By October 5, 1866, "end 'o track" was 247 miles out of Omaha, and the first Great Pacific Railroad Excursion left New York City to bring people out to see the "magic railroad" on the plains. While these sightseers were traveling west, "end 'o track" moved ahead another 32 miles.

The construction year of 1866 ended on December 11 with the startling record of 260 miles of track laid in exactly eight months — which more than met the terms of the Pacific Railroad Act. The UP's terminal base was at "Hell on Wheels" North Platte in Nebraska, a town that had sprung up overnight to provide entertainment for the workers and the soldiers who guarded them. North Platte was 293 miles from Omaha, and its "end 'o track" was 12 miles farther west.

During the winter of 1866–67, Dodge made plans for another leap ahead — 288 miles to Fort Sanders at the south end of the Laramie Plains. He announced this goal in a letter to his friend, General Sherman. The general, who earlier had scoffed at the idea of a Pacific railroad, sent this reply to Dodge: "I have just read with intense interest your letter of the 14th. Although you wanted me to keep it to myself, I believe you will sanction my sending it to General Grant. . . . It is almost a miracle to grasp your proposition to finish at Fort Sanders this year, but you have done so much that I mistrust my own judgment and accept yours."

Above: Cheyenne Indians attacking a UP hand car (from a contemporary painting). Below: A typical construction train. Workers lived in and on top of the long cars, which moved forward as the building progressed.

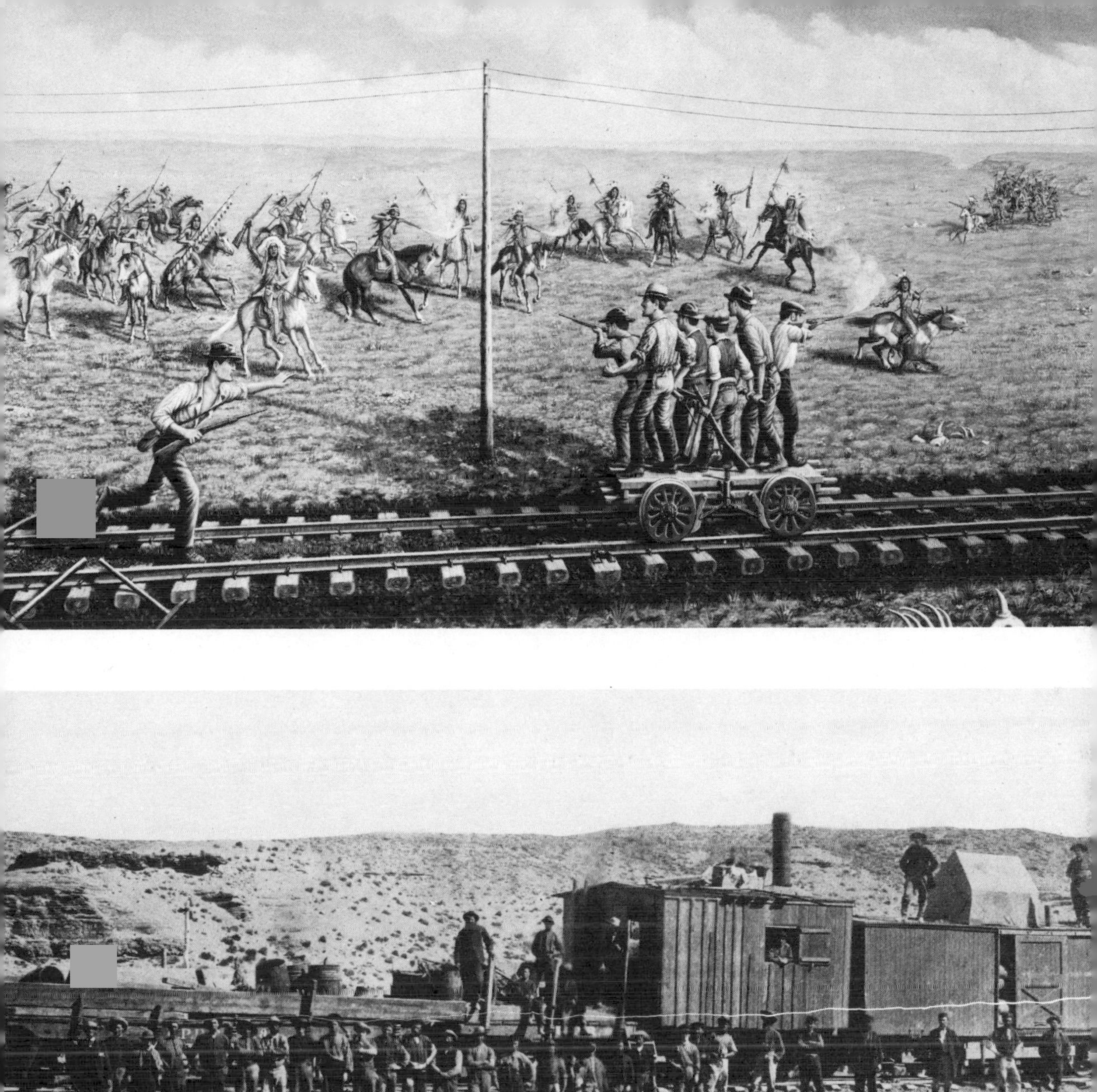

Dodge had good reason to be confident. The Chicago and Northwestern Railroad, building across Iowa, was approaching Council Bluffs, opposite Omaha. Soon there would be a rail connection between the Missouri River and Chicago. Furthermore, work on a bridge over the Missouri at Omaha was being started, and the company hoped to open it to traffic by the end of 1867. A rail connection and a bridge would be a big help to Dan Casement, who was working day and night to rush supplies westward.

Into the Sierras

On May 10, 1865, before the Union Pacific track layers had spiked down their first rail, the Central Pacific tracks were in Auburn, 5 miles east of Newcastle. In another month, they had reached Clipper Gap, another 7 miles, or 43 miles from Sacramento. The road was now heading into the main foothills of the Sierra Nevada, which forced the builders to make deep cuts and sweeping detours to keep the grade from becoming too steep for locomotives to climb.

Two more months were needed to push the track 11 miles to Illinois Town (present-day Colfax), which was another 500-foot climb from Clipper Gap. Here, on September 10, 1865, was "end 'o track." The year's record — 23 miles of track laid — did not impress the public. Aside from the difficult terrain, the labor problem had caused many delays. White laborers in California saw no reason to swing a pick or shovel for $1 to $2 a day when a man could earn $4 a day on the docks or in the mines and might even strike it rich on a gold or silver claim. Many workers accepted transportation on the railroad to a CP work camp only to keep on going to the mines. During one gold rush, two thousand laborers were shipped to the railroad camps before a hundred stayed to work.

Charles Crocker's answer to the labor problem was to call for Chinese coolies. The shipment of Chinese to San Francisco to serve as cooks, house boys, gardeners, and laundrymen was a thriving business as early as 1855. And by 1866, between 65,000 and 70,000 Chinese were working in California. In the late spring of 1865, Crocker had brought in a trial group of fifty Chinese. Irish workers hooted at the coolies in their basket hats, floppy pantaloons, and blue blouses; most of them were under 5 feet tall

and averaged only 120 pounds. But when they went to work with their picks, shovels, baskets, and wheelbarrows, they proved as efficient and industrious as ants. They kept at it hour after hour, never stopping to gossip or smoke, pausing only to drink a cup of tea two or three times a day and then bouncing right back to work. At the end of the day, the coolies' roadbed was longer and smoother than that of any white crew. Critics called them "Crocker's pets," and there was an uproar against this "invasion of yellow labor," but in the fall of 1865, Crocker had some three thousand of them at work.

To the Chinese, "Mistuh Clockee" was the man whose word was law, and they were ready to tackle any job he gave them at $1 a day. When Crocker decided to make stonemasons out of some Chinese, skeptical Superintendent J. H. Strobridge protested: "Make masons out of Chinese?"

"Sure," replied Crocker. "Didn't they build the Great Wall of China, the biggest piece of masonry in the world?" The Chinese proved to be good masons as well as excellent blacksmiths.

Commented President Stanford on the Chinese: "Quiet, peaceable, industrious and economical — ready and apt to learn all the different kinds of work required in railroad building, the Chinese were as efficient as white laborers. Without them it would be impossible to complete the western portion of this great national highway within the time required by the acts of Congress."

"End 'o track" remained at Colfax during the fall and winter of 1865, but grading, bridging, trestling, and tunneling crews pushed ahead toward the summit of the towering Sierra Nevada 50 miles away. Workers built a high curving trestle 1,100 feet long over deep gorges and ravines. Then they faced the biggest

Old print (above) and actual photo (below) of crews at work laying track on the Union Pacific in 1866.

Chinese laborers on a hand cart along the Central Pacific.

obstacle of all — a giant cliff called Cape Horn. A roadbed had to be carved out of the face of this granite cliff, and workers would have to dangle by ropes while they hammered and drilled and blasted 2,500 feet above the American River. The Chinese asked for this job and Crocker, ignoring the snorting disbelief of white workers, put the coolies to work on it late in 1865. The Chinese conquered Cape Horn by weaving baskets of reeds in which workers were lowered down the face of the cliff. They drilled, placed powder charges, lit fuses, and were then hauled up to the top.

In May, 1866, men could walk four abreast along Cape Horn's face, and on July 4, the track had reached the mining camp of Dutch Flat. That same day, the bore for the 508-foot Grizzly Hill Tunnel was completed 10 miles farther east. Completion of this tunnel put an end to talk by the CP's enemies that the road would end at Dutch Flat and that it would never meet the Union Pacific building from the East.

The track pushed on. Crocker saw to it that the grade was ready and the trestles, fills, bridges, and tunnels were prepared and waiting for the track layers. "I used to go up and down the road like a mad bull," said Crocker, "stopping along the way wherever there was anything amiss and raising Old Nick with the boys who were not up to time."

Cisco, located 15 miles east of Dutch Flat at about a 6,000-foot altitude, was reached on November 24, 1866. Cisco, named for John J. Cisco, assistant treasurer of the United States and first treasurer of the UP, was the terminus of the CP for nine months while the crowbars, hand drills, and gunpowder of the grading and tunneling crews broke a way for the rails through the giant Sierras. From Cisco, the summit of the Sierra Nevada was 14 miles away. Snows were 12 to 60 feet deep and the drifts remained from one winter to the next. The conquest of the Sierras

Some of Crocker's Chinese workers near the entrance to Summit Tunnel in 1866.

was considered the most difficult feat of railroad building in the world. Because of impossible canyons and gorges, fifteen tunnels would be required — ten on the west slope and five on the east. The longest tunnel — 1,659 feet — would bore through the summit of the Sierras.

Crocker had sent five hundred Chinese out in the spring of 1866 to begin the drilling on the Summit Tunnel. The rock was so hard that the shots of gunpowder merely spurted out of the holes, leaving the rock practically intact. The drilling proceeded at a rate of only 7 to 8 inches a day until nitroglycerine was used, but this proved almost as dangerous to the men as to the rock. While inspecting the Summit Tunnel, Strobridge was blinded in one eye by a delayed nitro blast. To speed the work, Chief Engineer Montague decided to sink a center shaft that would enable the Chinese to drill and blast in both directions from the middle to meet crews drilling in from the east and west.

The Terrible Winter of 1866-67

The winter of 1866–67 brought record snows. One storm followed another until the snow was 20 feet deep on level stretches. Half of the CP's force of ten thousand Chinese and whites was put to work shoveling it away.

On the railroad right-of-way through the timber, the Chinese choppers and stump grubbers worked in snow 4 feet deep. An avenue 200 feet wide had to be opened and the stumps grubbed out with pick and gunpowder to a width of 20 feet before the roadbed could go through. "Those are not Yankee forests," reported Assistant Engineer Clement, "but forests with trees four, six and eight feet in diameter." The Chinese chopped down the giant redwood and spruce trees, cut them into 15-foot lengths, and then blew out the stumps with kegs of gunpowder.

The snows continued day after day, and the tunnel men had to dig through 20 to 100 feet of drift before they reached the face of a cliff. Shut off from the world by giant drifts, they burrowed like gophers. At Tunnel No. 9, the trail down from the camp grew so dangerous due to snowslides that all work was halted. Slides carried away camps and crews. In the spring, the frozen corpses of Chinese were revealed — still upright with their

Above, an early Central Pacific "bucker" type snowplow near Cisco during the terrible winter of 1866–7. Below, the interior of a snowshed. Such sheds covered not only the main line but sidings and whole towns.

picks, drills, or hammers in their hands. The phrase "not a Chinaman's chance" was coined during that terrible winter. More than 500 Chinese, overworked and underpaid, were killed in two years.

The snows continued and working space became cramped because of the huge drifts. The impatient Crocker loaded his extra workers, their tools, and supplies on ox-team sleds and sent them over the Sierras and down the eastern slope of the mountains to begin grading in the Truckee River Valley near the Nevada line. He followed them with track equipment — 40 miles of rails, ties, and fastenings — plus forty freight cars and three locomotives, which he loaded on huge log skids swabbed with lard. Ox teams and hundreds of Chinese dragged these skids over the Sierras through snow 18 feet deep on the level and 40 to 60 feet deep in the drifts.

While workers graded and laid rails in the Truckee Valley, other crews finished the tunnels in the Sierras. In August, 1867, a locomotive crossed the Sierras through the Summit Tunnel. At the close of the construction year of 1867, "end 'o track" had moved out of Cisco, 16 miles over the Sierras summit and 10 miles down the eastern side. In the Truckee Valley, the rails stretched for 24 miles and crossed into Nevada. A gap of 7 miles in the mountains remained to be built after the tunnels on the eastern side of the Sierras were finished.

Crocker and Chief Engineer Montague now realized that the only way the CP could keep trains running during the winter was to build snowsheds over the tracks. These vast, peak-roofed wooden tunnels, looking like the covered bridges over rivers in the East, stretched for 37 miles, and cost from $10,000 to $30,000 a mile. Begun in 1867, they were completed in the summer of 1868. Some of the snowsheds had to be protected by huge stone walls built 50 feet uphill to fend off snowslides and floods during the spring. Hundreds of Chinese stonemasons worked in deep caverns dug out of the snow drifts to build the walls during the winter of 1867–68.

The Central Pacific had reached the California-Nevada state line ahead of the Union Pacific — but it was not content to stop there. The mines of Nevada might not hold out, and the agriculture of the rich Salt Lake Valley in Utah promised steady business for the CP. By an act of 1866, Congress specifically authorized the CP "to locate, construct and continue their road eastward, in a continuous line, until they shall meet and connect with the Union Pacific Railroad." Already CP engineer-surveyors had been running lines into Nevada and Utah. In the spring of 1867, CP engineers crossed the Wasatch range and moved on to Fort Bridger on the eastern slope of the Uintah-Wyoming range, setting their flags and stakes beside those of the Union Pacific engineers.

During the winter of 1867–68, CP graders pushed 20 miles into Nevada, or beyond Reno. Early in the spring of 1868, thousands of Chinese and Irish were put to work shoveling 30-foot drifts of snow and ice off the CP tracks in the mountains. These frozen drifts had defied snowplows pushed by several locomotives, and the workers had to blast them with gunpowder or nitro. Engineers cursed this stubborn snow and decided that snowsheds, even at $30,000 a mile, were cheap at double the price.

In May, 1868, the Central's Nevada tracks entered Reno. On June 15, the 7-mile gap in the mountains had been closed with rails. Soon trains were hauling 500 tons of rails and other equipment down the eastern slopes of the Sierras. The CP's Chinese and Irish pushed through the Truckee and moved toward the valley of the Humboldt to challenge the UP.

The UP's Bloody Year

While the Central Pacific was conquering the snows and granite walls of the Sierra Nevada, the Union Pacific was fending off widespread attacks by the Plains Indians. In 1867, the Sioux and Cheyenne made one last effort to halt the advancing rails of the UP. Generals Sherman and Grant both had promised their friend Dodge that the Army would protect the railroad builders, but Congress had drastically cut the size of the Army after the Civil War and economy was the watchword in Washington.

Between Omaha and Denver, Colorado, there were only some two hundred cavalrymen and six hundred infantrymen on duty. One supposedly important Army post, Fort Kearney in Nebraska, had a garrison of twelve infantrymen and a half-dozen musicians. Frustrated Army officers summed up their problem by saying: "It is hard to surround three Indians with one soldier." The situation would have been much more critical on the UP had it not been for the Pawnee scouts, led by their white chief, Major Frank North. He had organized them, and they trusted him because he spoke their language and lived in their lodges. They were outfitted with regulation Army weapons and clothing, but there all resemblance between the Pawnee and white soldiers ended. The Pawnee cut the seats out of their blue trousers and preferred to ride pantsless when they went into battle. Their disdain for discipline outraged Army officers, but when these Pawnee spotted their long-time enemies, the Sioux and Cheyenne, they fought with reckless bravery.

Dodge and Jack Casement organized the UP's tough ex-soldiers in the grading camps and had them build dugouts in the ground for protection in case of an Indian attack. The Casement construction train, called a "traveling arsenal," could arm hun-

Cheyenne Indians tearing up railroad tracks near Fossil Creek (now Russell), Kansas.

dreds of men at a moment's notice, but the engineers in the surveying parties hundreds of miles westward were sitting ducks for the Indians. As soon as survey work began in the early spring of 1867, Assistant Engineer H. H. Hills was killed and his surveying party was saved only by the quick thinking and organizing ability of an axman named J. M. Eddy.

Dodge was about to start west on an inspection trip with a party of distinguished guests when he heard of Hills's death and the good work of Eddy. He took his guests along to meet Eddy, figuring that from this man they would have a good chance to learn about the problems of building a railroad in Indian country. Final surveys had to be run through the most difficult and dangerous parts of the UP route — from the high plains of southeastern Wyoming, then in Nebraska Territory; over the Black Hills of the Laramie Plains; then on to the Red Desert and the Bitter Creek region; and over the snowy Wasatch range and westward to Great Salt Lake in Utah. The UP's graders were pressing close behind the engineers' survey stakes, and the track layers were at the graders' heels.

Among the guests in Dodge's party were Brevet Major General John A. Rawlins, chief of staff to General Grant in the Civil War; engineer Jacob Blickensderfer, Jr.; consulting engineer Silas Seymour of New York; and geologist David Van Lennep. General Rawlins, who was afflicted with tuberculosis, had been added to the inspection party at the personal request of General Grant in the hope that the trip would benefit his health. Blickensderfer had been ordered by President Andrew Johnson to determine the true eastern base of the Rocky Mountains, at which point the Union Pacific would begin to draw its $48,000-a-mile loan bonds from the government.

The Central Pacific's slick maneuver in getting President Lincoln to approve the moving of the Sierra Nevada range 24 miles west had become a joke in Congress, and President Johnson was determined that the UP would not have a chance to try to "move" the Rockies east in order to collect more loan bonds. Seymour, who was on hand to look and report back to his boss, Dr. Durant, was also to aid Blickensderfer in locating the foot of the Rockies. Geologist Van Lennep was on hand to locate veins of coal that could later replace wood as fuel for locomotives and also to spot supplies of stone to be used in ballasting the tracks.

Dodge soon met the survivors of Hills's surveying party and learned that J. M. Eddy had enlisted in the Thirteenth Illinois Volunteer Infantry at 16 and served in the Sixteenth Army Corps commanded by Dodge during the war. Eddy was promoted to higher rank in the surveying party and later became an engineer on the UP. When Dodge later took over as chief engineer of the Texas Pacific Railroad, in the 1870's, he hired Eddy as an engineer.

Late in June, the Dodge inspection party reached Crow Creek, which was renamed Cheyenne. July 4 was celebrated there and, a few days later, the Cheyenne Indians christened the town named for them by attacking a grading camp and killing five men. General Rawlings led a cavalry detachment to the rescue of the survivors.

While in Cheyenne, Dodge checked the line that James Evans had run through Lone Tree Pass and named it Evans Pass in his honor. Durant's man, Silas Seymour, kept prowling around looking for a "more suitable route" than the one that Evans had surveyed and Dodge had approved.

At Fort Sanders near Laramie, the telegraph brought Dodge news that Assistant Engineer Percy Browne's party had been attacked in the Red Desert west of the Laramie Plains and that Browne had been killed. Dodge went out to meet the Browne survey party, reorganized it, and then pushed on west. Near present-day Creston in the Red Desert, Dodge met the Thomas

H. Bates survey party. Bates's men had been without water for three days, had lost their horses, and were crawling on their hands and knees when rescued.

Dodge's inspection party finally reached Salt Lake City, where they were entertained by Brigham Young, president of the Mormon Church. During conferences with Young, who was anxious to have the Union Pacific run to Salt Lake City, Dodge heard reports that Crocker of the CP was boasting that his Chinese would lay a mile of track a day across the Nevada desert. This pace, said Young, would bring the CP into Salt Lake City by the summer of 1869. Then he looked expectantly at Dodge, who found himself on the spot. Surveys had indicated to him that the best route was north of Great Salt Lake, bypassing Salt Lake City, which would be reached by a branch line like that from Cheyenne to Denver. Dodge kept quiet about the UP surveys. All he could hope was that the Central Pacific's engineers also would agree that the best route was north of the lake. Wisely, he switched the subject by discussing Young's proposal to handle grading in Utah for the Union Pacific.

While Dodge's inspection party was moving west, the Sioux and Cheyenne were busy far to the east harassing Union Pacific workers. One group of warriors tried to capture an iron horse by stretching a 40-foot leather rope across the track. The two Indians nearest the track were swept under the locomotive's wheels and the others staggered back to camp with assorted bruises. Other Sioux and Cheyenne war parties raced trains, peppering locomotives and cars with rifle fire.

Then, on August 6, 1867, Chief Turkey Foot's Cheyenne warriors scored a victory over the iron horse — the first train wreck ever achieved by Indians. Near Plum Creek, some 230 miles west of Omaha, the Indians ripped up rails and fastened a tie to the track with telegraph wire. William Thompson, head

How the end of Union Pacific track looked in 1867 near Archer, Wyoming. Wagon train supplies have just caught up with the railroad workers.

lineman, and five of his crew were sent from Plum Creek station on a handcar to investigate the interruption of telegraph service. The handcar struck the tie, turned a somersault, and scattered the six men all over the prairie. A mounted Indian chased Thompson, shot him through the arm, felled him with his rifle, and then ripped off his scalp. Amazingly Thompson lived through the ordeal and later said: "It felt like the whole top of my head was taken right off." When the Indian rode away, the scalp slipped from his belt and Thompson retrieved it. Meanwhile, his companions were captured and killed.

The Cheyenne then piled more ties on the track and waited. A westbound train hit the ties and was derailed. The engineer and fireman were killed, but a man in the train's caboose sprinted back up the track with a lantern and warned another freight train. It reversed its engine and sped back to Plum Creek.

Next, the Indians ripped open boxcars containing calico, cottons, bonnets, hats, and food supplies. William Thompson, his scalp in hand, crouched nearby and watched the warriors race wildly across the prairie trailing strips of calico and cotton and tossing bonnets and hats in the air. Major North's Pawnee scouts, though more than 100 miles away, arrived the next day to track down and kill several of the Cheyenne. Thompson showed up later in Omaha, his scalp in a pail of water. Doctors tried to sew it back on his head but the operation was not successful.

The "Hell on Wheels" Towns

Even Indian attacks did not slow down Jack Casement's tough track layers. By June, 1867, 70 more miles of track had been spiked down. The terminus base now was new Julesburg, Nebraska, 377 miles from Omaha, and just across the Platte River from the old Overland Stage station of the same name. "Hell on Wheels" Julesburg was controlled by gamblers and cutthroats and was called the "wickedest city in America." Newspaperman Henry M. Stanley visited it and reported: "Watch-fires gleam over the sealike expanse of ground outside the city, while inside soldiers, herdsmen, teamsters, railroad men and women are dancing, singing and gambling. I verily believe that there are men here who would murder a fellow creature for five dollars. Nay, there are men who have already done it, and who stalk abroad in daylight unwhipped of justice. Not a day passes but a dead body is found somewhere in the vicinity with pockets rifled of their contents. . . ."

When Dodge returned from an inspection trip, Sam Reed told him of the shooting and knifing of UP workers. Dodge then had a quiet talk with Jack Casement. The next night, Casement handed out rifles to his toughest track layers and walked them slowly through town.

A few days later, Dodge asked Casement: "Are the gamblers quiet and behaving?"

"You bet they are, General," replied Casement. "They're out there in the graveyard."

On November 13, "end 'o track" reached Cheyenne, which

How a "hell on wheels" town looked on the Central Pacific in 1868 after the town had been laid out.

was proudly hailed as the "Magic City of the Plains." All Julesburg — merchants, saloonkeepers, gamblers, dance-hall girls, and cutthroats — moved to Cheyenne, leaving a station house and a litter of rubbish to mark the site of a town that had grown, flourished, and died in five months. Later, in 1881, present-day Julesburg, Colorado, was founded.

Cheyenne soon rivaled Julesburg as the stronghold of the lawless. When honest merchants complained, Colonel J. D. Stevenson of Fort Russell put Cheyenne under Army rule until a town government was elected. The new mayor-magistrate, Luke Murrin, ordered any man who indulged in gunplay within town limits to pay a $10 fine "whether he hit or missed."

After the Army withdrew its patrols from Cheyenne, the gamblers and cutthroats moved back into town and the cheating and killing resumed. Then a secret "citizens' committee" went into action and hanged at least twelve men. As the rails marched on westward, most of the gamblers and other crooks moved on to the new "Hell on Wheels" towns and Cheyenne quieted down.

Cheyenne, 517 miles west of Omaha, was selected as the junction for Denver, from which the Denver Pacific Railroad was soon to build northward. A week was spent building sidings and switches and laying foundations for the shops and roundhouse. Then the track layers headed eagerly for the Black Hills. The summit was but 30 miles away, and Fort Sanders, Dodge's goal for 1867, was only another 20 miles beyond. However, interference from Dr. Durant in New York stalled the track layers. Durant's man, Silas Seymour, changed the route through the Black Hills that had been approved by Dodge. December snows caught the workers at 8,000 feet, high up in the pass. "End 'o track" was halted 10 miles from the summit and 30 miles from Fort Sanders. But 240 miles of track had been laid in 1867, and the world's records in track construction had been broken by the laying of 2½ miles a day and 150 miles in 100 days.

While Jack Casement's workers waited for spring, Dan Casement kept the supplies moving out of Omaha. Cheyenne soon was filled with vast piles of rails and ties. The Casements' portable warehouses, which could be taken down and assembled quickly at another supply point, were jammed with equipment and food and fodder for men and animals.

Eighteen hundred and sixty-eight was to be the year in which the UP fought it out with the CP. By holding out promises of bonds and land grants for each mile of track laid, the government had turned the construction of the Pacific railroad into a contest. The CP could build as far as it might beyond the California-Nevada border, and the UP could go as far west as its money and supplies would permit. The race appeared to favor the CP. It had to build some 600 miles to reach the Great Salt Lake. But it had already conquered the Sierra Nevada and would have an easier time laying track across the Nevada desert. The UP still had to build through the Wasatch chain of mountains, which it would reach in the winter of 1868.

During the winter of 1867–68, Dodge was called back to New York for an important conference with the Union Pacific directors. He was told that regardless of cost the UP rails had to beat those of the CP into Ogden, Utah, at the northern end of the Great Salt Lake. If the CP got there first, it could control traffic on the Pacific (transcontinental) railroad and shut the UP out of the Salt Lake Valley.

Showdown at Fort Sanders

Despite early spring snows and freezing winds, Casement's track layers crossed the summit of the Black Hills and pushed on to Laramie, "Gem City of the Plains," in one month. The track-laying pace picked up across the Laramie Plains and then slowed as the workers pushed into the bleak flatness of the Red Desert. Then summer laid a fiery blanket of heat over the men. "This land," said a sun-scalded Irishman, "is so dry that a jack rabbit has to carry a canteen and a haversack."

While Casement's men were battling the desert, Dodge and Reed were in Laramie fighting the latest schemes of Dr. Durant and Seymour. Dodge, who had been elected to the House of Representatives by his Iowa district, was in Washington when he received a message from Reed: "Urgent you be in Laramie May 16." Dodge arrived to find that Dr. Durant had ordered all work stopped on the shops and roundhouse in Cheyenne. He planned to move them to Laramie. At the same time, Seymour had changed another route approved by Dodge on the ground that it would reduce grading and save money. Dodge snorted angrily. The Seymour route was 20 miles longer, another attempt by Dr. Durant to collect more bonds per mile from the government.

Dodge was caught in the middle of the feud between rival groups in the Union Pacific and the Credit Mobilier. One group was headed by Dr. Durant, who saw no hope of profit from the Union Pacific and bluntly said his idea was "to grab a wad of money from the construction fees — and get out." One way to do this was to change Dodge's route, make it longer, and collect more bonds per mile from the government.

The group fighting Dr. Durant was led by Oakes and Oliver Ames, shovel and tool manufacturers of Easton, Massachusetts, and Sidney Dillon of New York. During the gold rush of 1849, the Ameses' "Old Colony" shovels became famous for quality, and they were used by graders on the UP. In 1864, President Lincoln had appealed to Oakes Ames to back the Union Pacific, and he had responded by investing $1,000,000 of his own money in the road. The Ameses were willing to take profits from the Credit Mobilier, but they did not want to so burden the Union Pacific with debt that it could never be a good investment on its own.

In 1868, the Ames group had become more powerful in the Union Pacific and the Credit Mobilier, but it was never able to oust Dr. Durant from his position as vice-president and general manager of the UP. And Dr. Durant used his position to snipe continually at Dodge, who had the confidence of the Ameses. In switching the railroad shops from Cheyenne to Laramie, Seymour argued that Laramie was a better location. This suited Dr. Durant because real estate sales in Cheyenne had lagged, and a shift of the shops to Laramie would boost land sales there.

Dodge's first move when he got to Laramie was to telegraph the mayor of Cheyenne that the shops would stay in that town. Then he went out looking for Dr. Durant. Dodge met him in the middle of Laramie's main street and roared: "You are now going to learn that the men working for the Union Pacific will take orders from me and not from you! If you interfere, there will be trouble — trouble from the Government, from the Army and from the men themselves!"

A portrait of Oakes Ames who, with his brother Oliver, was a formidable financial backer of the Union Pacific.

General Ulysses S. Grant and his party at the Fort Sanders meeting, just south of Laramie, Wyoming, 1868, on the Union Pacific. Grant, then a nominee for the Presidency, stands at left center with his hands on the fence. Dodge stands at extreme left. Next but one to him is General Phil Sheridan (hands in pockets). General William T. Sherman stands at center, with coat over arm.

Dr. Durant flushed angrily and pulled at his neat Vandyke beard. "We shall see," he said as he walked away.

News of the Dodge-Durant showdown in Laramie reached New York in a few days. Oakes Ames and Sidney Dillon immediately went to Washington to discuss the railroad's problems with General Sherman. Then they went back to New York to confront Dr. Durant when he returned from Laramie. They told Durant that Seymour's changes in Dodge's routes had been called a deliberate attempt to obtain more government bonds and land grants. Ames added that the decision to shift the shops from Cheyenne to Laramie could cause a lot of trouble. He pointed out that Congress soon would pass a bill creating Wyoming Territory with Cheyenne as its capital. How popular would the Union Pacific be with territorial officials after it moved the railroad shops out of the capital city?

Dr. Durant refused to budge. He said Seymour was a better engineer than Dodge, and he planned to ask the directors of the Union Pacific to fire Dodge. Ames then shook Durant up a bit by telling him that General Grant would be in Laramie in July during the treaty talks with the Sioux Indians. Grant also wanted to inspect the Union Pacific tracks in Wyoming and hear both sides of the Dodge-Durant disagreement. He expected Durant and Seymour to meet him at Fort Sanders, near Laramie, in late July.

On July 26, 1868, at Fort Sanders, Wyoming Territory, Army officers and government and railroad officials met to settle the Dodge-Durant feud. The referee was to be General Grant, then the Republican party nominee for President. Grant was still a private citizen, but he was expected to win the presidency in November, and his word would carry much weight. Dr. Durant still felt he was in a strong bargaining position. Horatio Seymour, brother of Silas Seymour, was the Democratic candidate for President, and if Grant favored Dodge over Durant and Silas Seymour, the Democrats could do a lot of talking about it during the campaign.

Before the meeting started, a photographer arranged the members of Grant's party for a picture in front of the house of Colonel John Gibbon, commanding officer at Fort Sanders. Dodge commented later that "probably no more noted military gathering has occurred since the Civil War." There were General Philip Sheridan, commanding the Military Division of Missouri; General William T. Sherman, commander in chief of the Army; General Frederick T. Dent, Grant's brother-in-law and West Point classmate; General August Kautz, who in 1865 led black troops into Richmond, Virginia. Among the civilians were Jesse L. Williams, the government commissioner for the Union Pacific, and Dr. Durant, Seymour, Sidney Dillon, and Dodge of the Union Pacific.

Grant opened the meeting by pointing out that in the recent treaty signed at Laramie the government had agreed to withdraw troops from forts Phil Kearny and Reno and keep white men out of the Big Horn country in return for Sioux chief Red Cloud's promise to halt attacks on the Union Pacific's workers. At the same time, said Grant, the government expected the officials of the Union Pacific to stop fighting among themselves and get on with the business of building a railroad. Grant then asked Dr. Durant to state his case.

Dr. Durant charged that Dodge had selected an "impossible route," had wasted money, and failed to locate the road into Salt Lake City. Grant took his ever-present cigar out of his mouth, studied it a moment, and said, "What about that, Dodge?"

Dodge carefully discussed the changes that Durant and Seymour had ordered while he was in Washington and explained why it was not wise from an engineering standpoint to run the line to Salt Lake City. "The government commissioners," said

Dodge, "complain of changes in the railroad route. They dislike to approve a line unless they know it is a sound line, built for traffic and not just to get subsidy money from the Government. I want the road to be safe, and I want it as straight as it can be built. I cannot have financial interests dictating the layout of the line. As to that, neither Durant nor any other man will interfere as long as I am chief engineer. If change is insisted upon, I'll quit."

Grant sat quietly for many seconds, puffing his cigar. Dr. Durant's thin fingers pulled nervously at his Vandyke. Finally, Grant spoke:

"The Government expects this railroad to be finished. The Government expects the railroad company to meet its obligations. And the Government expects General Dodge to remain with the road as its chief engineer until it is completed."

General Sherman smiled grimly and looked at Dr. Durant, whose face colored with anger — but only for an instant. Dr. Durant leaped to his feet and smilingly extended his hand to Dodge: "I withdraw my objections," said Durant. "We all want Dodge to stay with the road."

The meeting quickly broke up and members of Grant's party moved out to a special train that waited to take them to Medicine Bow, out on the Laramie Plains. At Laramie, everyone turned out to cheer Grant, and a band blasted its greeting into the hot afternoon. Grant spoke briefly, and the train moved westward where the workers, Union and Confederate veterans alike, cheered Grant, Sherman, and Sheridan. The special train ended its run at Medicine Bow, and Dodge boarded a construction train for Benton, the newest "Hell on Wheels" town.

"As far as you could see around Benton," wrote a reporter, "not a green tree, shrub or spear of grass was visible; the red hills, scorched and bare as if blasted by the lightnings of an angry god, bounded the white basin on the north and east, while to the south

Benton, Wyoming Territory, 1868 — the "hell on wheels town" of which it was said that, "it grew in a day and vanished in a night, but was red hot while it lasted . . ."

and west spread the gray desert till it was interrupted by another range of red and yellow hills."

Benton's streets were 8 inches deep in white dust, and buildings, tents, and brush shacks were blanketed with it. Water hauled 3 miles from the North Platte River sold for $3 a barrel and 10 cents a bucket. Merchants put up fake brick and brownstone buildings of painted pine, shipped from Chicago at $300 delivered. A half-dozen men could erect a business block in a day. Two boys with screwdrivers could assemble a fancy dwelling in three hours. But the rails pushed rapidly on, and in sixty days all that remained of Benton were a few barrels, rusty tin cans, chimneys, and one hundred nameless graves.

In August, the rails swept across the Red Desert and climbed the broad, bare plateau of the Continental Divide at a height of 7,164 feet. Then they charged on into the alkali dust of the aptly named Bitter Creek Basin. For 100 miles around, the water was poisoned by salt and alkali. It foamed in the locomotive boilers and ate at the stomachs of the workers. Men took what water they could get, hauled by wagon from 2 to 10 miles away. The sun struck men down by day; at night, water froze in the camp buckets.

Back east, people were following the exploits of Casement's ironmen as eagerly as people today follow the flights of our astronauts. Big-city newspapers displayed a bulletin in each issue: "one and nine-tenths miles of track laid yesterday on the Union Pacific"; "two miles of track laid yesterday on the Union Pacific"; "two and three-quarters miles of track laid yesterday on the Union Pacific."

Winter Ordeal

Late in September, 1868, Casement's tireless ironmen left the desolate Bitter Creek region behind and pushed up the slopes of the Uintah range. Signs of an early winter were in the biting wind, and reports from Nevada indicated that the Central Pacific's Chinese were laying rails at a rate that might bring them into Ogden ahead of the Union Pacific. Also nagging Dodge, Reed, and Casement was the "Mormon problem." President Brigham Young of the Mormon Church would soon have to be told that the UP could not build into Salt Lake City. If this news caused Young to oppose the UP, it would have a difficult time laying track through Utah. Mormon workers were needed for grading, and Utah was a rich storehouse of farm produce and hay; in fact, it was the only one in the 1,700 miles between Omaha and the Sierra Nevada.

Accordingly, Dodge went to Salt Lake City and told Young the bad news. The Mormon leader stormed from the room and on Sunday preached a sermon at the Tabernacle in which he denounced both Dodge and the Union Pacific. A few days later, Dodge went back to Young with a report showing that the Central Pacific's engineers also opposed running a line south of the lake to Salt Lake City. The next Sunday, Young preached another sermon and said that the Union Pacific was probably Utah's best friend. He then told Dodge he was prepared to furnish labor to grade a roadbed 200 miles east and west of Great Salt Lake.

Reports that the CP's Chinese had laid down more than 5 miles of track in a day aroused Jack Casement. He gave the appropriate orders, and the UP's ironmen slammed down 6 miles of track from dawn to dusk. Then the Chinese came back with 7 miles in a day, and at Granger, Wyoming, late in October, Casement's men spiked down 7½ miles. Whereupon, Charles Crocker of the CP announced: "The Central Pacific promises ten miles in one working day." When Dr. Durant heard this boast, he wired: "Ten thousand dollars that you can't do it before witnesses."

"We'll notify you," wired Crocker.

Out of Granger, Casement's hurrying ironmen pushed "end 'o track" 8 more miles into Utah Territory. Speed was now the watchword, and little time was being spent making a smooth roadbed and ballasting the ties with rock. The ties were laid over the clods turned by the graders' picks and shovels and the rails were spiked down. Government Director Jesse L. Williams, whose job it was to oversee and approve the work on the UP, explained: "The first object in railroad construction is, very properly, to lay the rails so that material can be hauled to the road builders."

At Piedmont, the rails touched the top of the Uintah chain of the northern Wasatch range. Here were the great stacks of ties that had been cut in the mountains and then floated down streams and gathered at Tie Siding. Here, too, the Credit Mobilier went broke. Oakes and Oliver Ames scraped up money from somewhere and the work went on. Oakes Ames wired Dodge: "Go ahead. Stand by the company and let the Ameses take care of themselves. The work shall not stop even if it takes the shovel shop." Dodge later declared: "Nothing but the pluck of the Ameses, fortified with their extensive credit . . . carried the road through." When Oakes Ames died, his company was burdened with debts he had incurred helping to finance the Union Pacific.

Dodge now ordered Jack Casement to take over the grading as well as the track laying. In the past, when grading contractors had failed to finish a job in time, Casement's ironmen had completed the work. Now, the ironmen got welcome help when Mormon men and boys with picks, shovels, and wheelbarrows took over the grading from Echo Canyon to Promontory Summit, west of Great Salt Lake. They went at their task with a will and a song:

At the head of great Echo, the railway's begun,
The Mormons are cutting and grading like fun;
They say they'll stick to it until it's complete —
When friends and relations they're hoping to meet.
Hurrah, hurrah, the railroad's begun,
Three cheers for the contractor, his name's Brigham Young.
Hurrah, Hurrah, we're honest and true,
And if we stick to it, it's bound to go through.

The Union Pacific paid $10 a day and keep for a man and ox team, and graders got up to $3 a day. Mormon farmers sold hay for $100 a ton and potatoes at $7 a bushel. At the completion of the railroad, the UP owed Young $1,000,000, and he frequently thundered in the Tabernacle at the railroad's failure to pay its debts. Part of the final settlement of his claim consisted of leftover equipment that Young used for his Utah Central Railroad. At Aspen station, 9½ miles beyond Piedmont, Casement's ironmen found themselves at 7,540 feet, an elevation second only to the summit of the Black Hills (now called Sherman Summit). Plunging down from this height, the tracks reached Bear River, crossed it on a trestle 600 feet long and moved on to Evanston, where the snow already was banked 6 feet high. Finally, the track layers reached Wasatch, the winter terminus of the UP, 7,000 feet in the air and 966 miles from Omaha.

For three winter months, 4,000 brawling graders, track layers, and trainmen found what amusement they could in Wasatch. Of the forty-three people who went to the town graveyard, only five were said to have "died natural." Three of these had frozen to death while drunk; one, a girl, had inhaled charcoal fumes; and the other girl, chloroform.

In November, two locomotives were needed to push one snowplow. The workers said that they had to shovel down to find their tents, and they could get a clean shave by just sticking their faces out in the wind. But this was just the beginning of the UP's winter ordeal.

In late November, a blizzard whirled across the Wasatch peaks, burying the town in drifts 10 feet high, stalling trains, and snapping telegraph wires. Two days later, the operating department cleared enough of the road to free a half-dozen stormbound construction trains. Casement's ironmen grimly fought the snow and blizzard winds to lay track toward Echo Canyon, 4 miles from Wasatch and 700 feet lower. To cover that drop, Dodge's engineers had planned two high trestles across gullies and a tunnel 700 feet long through the shoulder of a ridge. The bridge gangs finished the trestles, but the tunnel crews were stalled. The men had to dig through frozen clay and sandstone that was as hard as granite, blasting it with nitroglycerine. Each yard of excavation cost $3.50, and the tunnel moved forward 1 foot a day.

Dodge, Reed, and Casement worriedly discussed the delay and decided that they could not wait for the tunnel. Reports told of the CP laying 2 to 3 miles of track a day across the Nevada desert. So Dodge approved the building of a zigzag temporary route, named a Z, over the ridge and down to the head of Echo Canyon. Casement's ironmen dropped ties on the ice and snow and spiked down the rails. The first train down the Z ripped up the track and slid 100 feet into the canyon bottom. The ironmen repaired the Z and another train loaded with rails safely made the trip down. On the canyon bottom, track was laid over ground so mushy that workers had to steady the rails with crowbars while trains, hurrying forward with supplies, passed by. Track layers and graders demanded $3.50 a day and got it. For Sunday work, they got $7.00.

Then a December blizzard smashed into Wasatch. The telegraph wires, recently repaired, went down again, and all traffic came to a halt. On Christmas Day, every door in Wasatch was frozen solid and 30 feet of snow covered the rails. On New Year's Day, the storm slackened, and snowplows hammered at the huge drifts. But the first week in January, another blizzard struck. The telegraph wires remained down, and 200 miles of track lay buried in snowdrifts. The UP failed to learn from the experience of the CP, which had built snowsheds to protect its track. While the UP was stalled, the CP later reported that none of its trains ran more than two hours late during the worst blizzards.

Casement's men opened the road back as far as the tunnel so the men there could continue to work. They also cleared off the buried Z. The savage cold cut through the heaviest clothing, and the men had to build a chain of bonfires to keep from freezing. Ties now costing $6 apiece were the only fuel. One worker estimated that he had warmed his hands over a $150 fire.

The track remained blocked with snow across the Laramie Plains, and no rails could reach Casement's ironmen. Dodge ordered the men to tear up the sidings and use those rails. Casement's ironmen backtracked all the way to Bear River, ripping up all the sidings that paralleled the main track. Trains then gingerly crept over the shaky Z and delivered rails to the impatient track layers.

Three weeks after Christmas, one of Dan Casement's supply trains broke through the snow blockade and hammered into Wasatch. The telegraph wires were repaired, and a message said that the CP was within 120 miles of Ogden. It had cut the UP's lead in half. But Casement's men hitched up their pants and vowed that

A construction train at Devil's Gate Bridge, a trestle on the approach to Promontory.

the Central would not beat them to Ogden. Down Echo Canyon the ironmen went, and through the Weber Gorge. Late in January, they passed a gaunt pine that displayed this sign: "1,000 Miles — from Omaha."

Now word came that in Washington Collis P. Huntington had boldly filed a claim to the right-of-way through Weber Gorge and Echo Canyon and claimed government bonds on it. He ignored the fact that the Central's track was still 100 miles from Ogden and that the UP, with 25 miles to go, had virtually won the race into Salt Lake Valley.

On the last day of President Andrew Johnson's administration, the bonds claimed by the CP were issued, and on that same day, March 3, 1869, the UP entered Ogden. The band from Fort Douglas blared a welcome and paraders bore the sign: "Hail to the Highway of the Nations! Utah Bids You Welcome!" That night Dodge told his engineers of the government's action favoring the CP. But he reminded them that the next day, March 4, Grant would become President and what Johnson had done, Grant could undo. He believed Grant would see to it that the UP was treated fairly. Meanwhile, if the CP intended to lay track east of Ogden, the UP would lay track west of Ogden and shut the CP out of that town.

Working day and night shifts, the UP track layers headed northwest along the lake and swung westward to climb the ridge to Promontory Summit. Across the desert west of Promontory, the Central was stalled by the wreck of a rail train that had plunged through a trestle. Smallpox also swept the CP camps. Crocker worked his Chinese by the light of sagebrush fires to make up for lost time.

Between Ogden and Promontory, the graders of the CP and UP began digging parallel roadbeds only a few hundred feet apart. Casement's white workers glared at the Chinese and laid a "grave" — a blast that buried several CP graders. Twice this was done despite stern orders from Dodge. So the Chinese laid a "grave" of their own — killing three UP workers and injuring others. This blast ended the macabre sport of "grave laying," which was becoming too costly.

Early in April, 1869, President Grant let it be known that the government was tired of having the UP and CP build a railroad that did not connect anywhere. Dodge, Dr. Durant, and Huntington then conferred and worked out a compromise. The Central agreed to stop at Promontory Point (or Summit) if the Union Pacific would sell its trackage from there east to Ogden. Moving out of Blue Creek, the UP workers built a trestle 300 feet long and 30 feet high, and another 500 feet long and 87 feet high to reach Promontory Summit. As the men labored, the UP engineers were thankful that all this work would be paid for by the CP. On April 28, the UP workers could see the glare of CP bonfires out in the desert to the west.

That same day, Crocker reminded Dr. Durant of his bet that the CP could not lay 10 miles of track in a day. On April 29, a handpicked gang of Crocker's workers laid 3,520 rails, with 55,000 spikes and 14,080 bolts from sunup to sundown for a total of 10 miles and 200 feet. The eight ironmen who handled the rails lifted a total 1,970,000 pounds. To avoid stirring up the white workers, no Chinese were used that day. The eight men who set the record — Mike Shay, Mike Kennedy, Mike Sullivan, Pat Joyce, Thomas Dailey, George Wyatt, Edward Killeen, and Fred McNamara — were Irish almost to a man. The UP engineers and workers protested that their 7½ miles had been laid without special preparations, as had been made by the CP. But since the CP had left the UP workers only 4 more miles of track to lay before the lines met at Promontory, there was nothing UP men could do but grumble.

The next day, the UP and CP workers leisurely laid track to the meeting place. On May 1, they stopped short by a pair of rails each. A mere 58 feet separated the two "ends 'o track." To the west, the rails ran 690 miles to Sacramento; to the east, they ran 1,086 miles to Omaha. In 13 months, the UP had laid 555 miles of main track and 180 miles of sidings and temporary track. The CP had laid 549 miles of main track. The track records were about the same, but the UP had faced the greater task, not only crossing the deserts in the summer but the snow-clogged mountains in the winter.

April 29, 1869, Camp Victory, Utah, near Promontory. On this day, Crocker's construction men set an all-time record by laying more than ten miles of track.

"The Last Spike Is Driven . . ."

Promontory, the last of the "Hell on Wheels" towns, did its best to dress up its drab shacks and buildings for the great moment — the meeting of the rails. By agreement between chief engineers Dodge and Montague, the ceremony was to take place Saturday, May 8.

A delegation of dignitaries from California was the first to arrive on the special train of President Leland Stanford of the CP. This train carried two important items: the Last Tie — of polished mahogany, 8 feet long, 8 inches wide, and 6 inches thick; bound with silver and set with a silver plate inscribed "The Last Tie Laid on the Completion of the Pacific Railroad, May __, 1869"; and the Last Spike, cast from $20 gold pieces and about 7 inches long. On the head of the spike was inscribed "The Last Spike"; on one side, "The Pacific Railroad. Ground Broken January 8, 1863, Completed May __, 1869"; on another side, "May God continue the unity of our country as this railroad unites the two great oceans of the world"; on the third face, "Presented by David Hewes, San Francisco"; on the fourth, the names of the company officers.

When the Leland Stanford train arrived, the Californians were told that the UP delegation would be late. Heavy rains had ripped up track east of Ogden. Casement's ironmen went to work repairing the track, and the train from the East reached Promontory on May 9. That night, Dodge gave a dinner for his engineers in the Lincoln Car.

May 10, 1869, was a cold, clear day, and a high wind whipped the bunting on the special trains gathered at Promontory Point. From the west moved the Central Pacific's Jupiter 60;

Above: After the last spike was driven at Promontory Point, the locomotives of the Union Pacific and Central Pacific were moved forward until their engineers could touch each other and champagne could be exchanged. Shaking hands in center are Grenville Dodge (right) and CP Chief Engineer Samuel Montague.

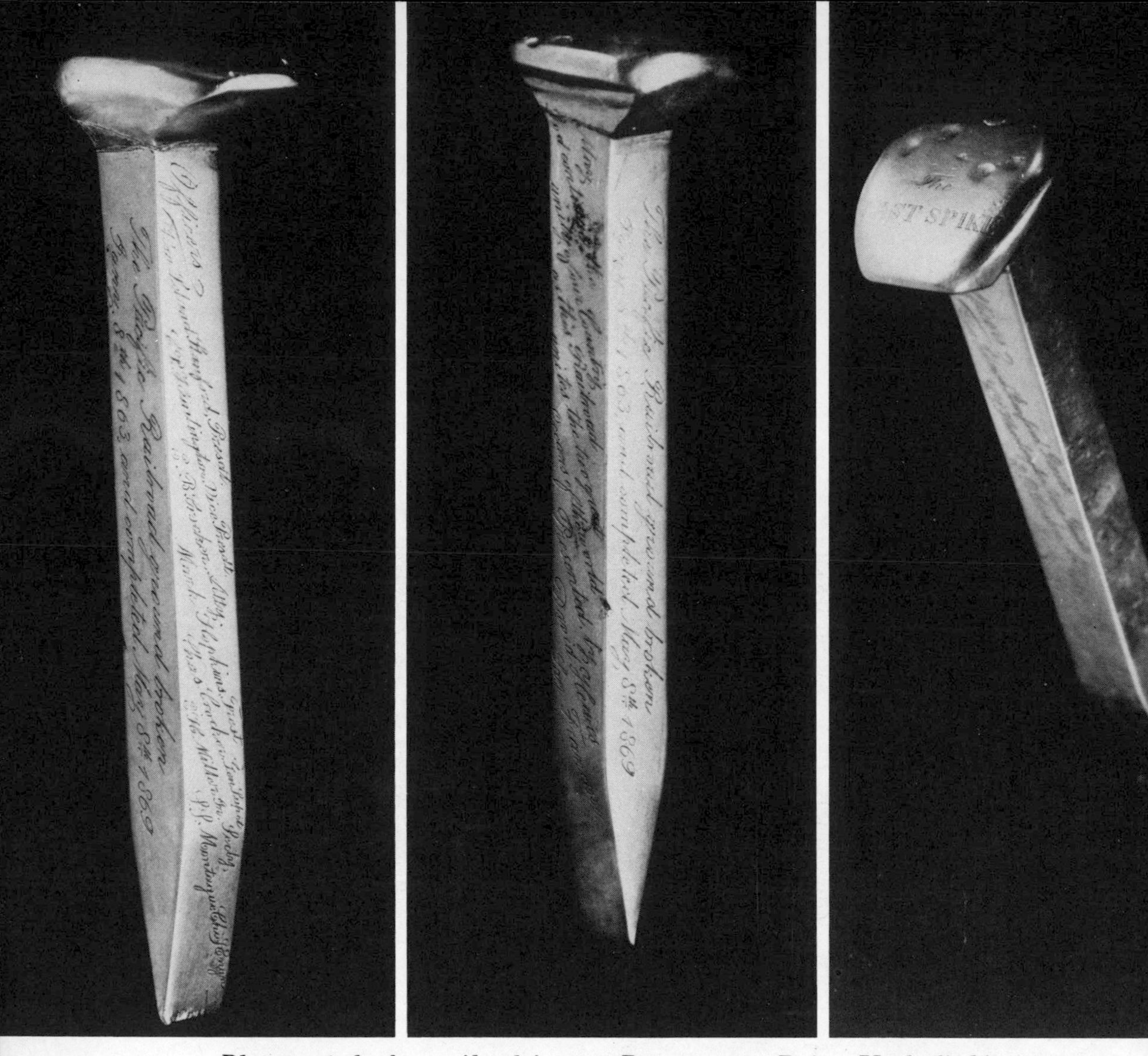

Photos of the last spike driven at Promontory Point, Utah, linking the transcontinental railroad. It was driven into a silver-plated tie made of laurel wood. Actually, both spike and tie were looted just after the ceremony for souvenirs and a common tie and iron spike substituted.

from the east moved the Union Pacific's 119. They halted a rail-length apart. Photographers scurried about, seeking the best place for their cameras. Construction superintendents Strobridge of the CP and Reed of the UP brought the silverplated tie from the Stanford train. The final two rails followed — the UP rail carried by an Irish squad under Foreman Guilford, and the CP rail carried by a squad of Chinese under their boss, H. H. Minkler.

As the two rails arrived, a man called to photographer Charles Savage: "Now's the time, Charley, take a shot!" The word "shot" startled the Chinese who had had their fill of the white man's violence in CP camps and terminal towns. They looked up, saw the opening of the camera pointed their way, and immediately dropped the rail and scattered while the crowd roared. After considerable argument, they finally came back and laid their rail.

A telegraph operator clicked a message to offices throughout the nation: "When the Last Spike is driven at Promontory Point, we will say, 'Done.' Don't break the circuit, but watch for the signals of the blows of the hammer."

After a prayer and short speeches by Stanford and Dodge, the telegrapher tapped: "All ready now. The spike will soon be driven. The signal will be three dots for the commencement of the blows."

The Last Spike was set in position and President Stanford stepped forward with a silver maul. He swung the maul — and missed. Stanford, a bit embarrassed, handed the maul to Dr. Durant. He swung and obligingly missed too. Meanwhile, the telegrapher had ignored the miss by Stanford and tapped: "Done." Throughout the country, bells pealed and cannon boomed while people paraded. At 12:47, the magnetic ball on the dome of the Capitol in Washington fell and the crowd roared its approval.

To President Grant went the formal announcement:

The last rail is laid, the last spike driven. The Pacific Railroad is completed. The Point of junction is 1,086 miles west of the Missouri River, and 690 miles east of Sacramento City.

LELAND STANFORD
CENTRAL PACIFIC RAILROAD

T. C. DURANT
SIDNEY DILLON
JOHN DUFF
UNION PACIFIC RAILROAD

President Stanford and Dr. Durant shook hands across the Last Tie while people cheered and locomotives shrieked. All the dignitaries were invited to tap the Last Spike, and it soon was in rather battered condition. The final setting of the spike was assigned to the two chief engineers, Dodge and Montague.

The two locomotives, Jupiter 60 and 119, now snorted forward and touched pilots (cowcatchers). Workers swarmed over them and broke bottles of champagne that foamed down onto the Last Tie and the Last Spike.

In San Francisco, Bret Harte, editor of the *Overland Monthly*, wrote a poem to accompany his next editorial:

What was it the engines said,
Pilots touching head to head,
Facing on a single track,
Half a world behind each back?"

When the locomotives backed away, UP and CP crews charged in, jerked out the Last Spike and Last Tie, placed another tie, and drove home iron spikes. As soon as the workers finished, souvenir hunters rushed at the tie with knives and axes. Over the years, six ties were demolished for souvenirs.

Aftermath: Glory and Scandal

Theodore D. Judah, whose dream of a transcontinental railroad came true, is a forgotten man today. And the Central Pacific, which Judah organized, is all but forgotten too. The CP gradually lost its identity after it and the Southern Pacific were combined in 1884. Now, when passengers ride Southern Pacific trains that cross the long grades and high trestles of the Sierras and thunder through tunnels and snowsheds, few think of the Central Pacific.

The Union Pacific, however, kept its identity and has been celebrated in books and motion pictures. It also attracted much unwelcome attention in the 1870's when Congress began an investigation of the Credit Mobilier. A scandal soon arose over the amount the directors of the Union Pacific had paid the Credit Mobilier to build the railroad. The profit of the construction company ranged from 25 to 200 percent, depending on how much the government bonds and the UP bonds and stock it received in payment were worth at the time. In 1868, UP bonds were worth around 45 to 50 cents on the dollar and its stock was worth only 30 cents on the dollar. Between 1867 and 1872, the UP paid out more money in interest on government and UP bonds than it made hauling freight and passengers.

Without excusing all of the slippery maneuvers of Dr. Durant of the UP and the Big Four of the Central Pacific, historians blame much of the waste and dishonesty in the building of the Pacific railroad on Congress and the federal government. They insist that the Pacific Railroad Act of 1862 was particularly unrealistic and sloppy legislation. It gave the CP and UP land grants, but much of this land would remain worthless until the railroads

1869. **May 10th.** 1869.

GREAT EVENT

Rail Road from the Atlantic to the Pacific

GRAND OPENING

OF THE

Union Pacific

RAIL ROAD,

PLATTE VALLEY ROUTE.

PASSENGER TRAINS LEAVE

OMAHA

ON THE ARRIVAL OF TRAINS FROM THE EAST.

THROUGH TO SAN FRANCISCO

In less than Four Days, avoiding the Dangers of the Sea!

Travelers for Pleasure, Health or Business

Will find a Trip over The Rocky Mountains Healthy and Pleasant.

LUXURIOUS CARS & EATING HOUSES

ON THE UNION PACIFIC RAIL ROAD.

PULLMAN'S PALACE SLEEPING CARS

RUN WITH ALL THROUGH PASSENGER TRAINS.

GOLD, SILVER AND OTHER MINERS!

Now is the time to seek your Fortunes in Nebraska, Wyoming, Arizona, Washington, Dakotah Colorado, Utah, Oregon, Montana, New Mexico, Idaho, Nevada or California.

CONNECTIONS MADE AT

CHEYENNE for DENVER, CENTRAL CITY & SANTA FE

AT OGDEN AND CORINNE FOR HELENA, BOISE CITY, VIRGINIA CITY, SALT LAKE CITY AND ARIZONA.

THROUGH TICKETS FOR SALE AT ALL PRINCIPAL RAILROAD OFFICES!

Be Sure they Read via Platte Valley or Omaha

Company's Office 72 La Salle St., opposite City Hall and Court House Square, Chicago.

CHARLES E. NICHOLS, Ticket Agent.

G. P. GILMAN, JOHN P. HART, J. BUDD, W. SNYDER,

completed their tracks. Furthermore, the government granted lands in alternate sections, retaining the sections between. The act also provided government loan bonds — but at 6 percent interest over a 30-year period. Since the government was able to borrow money at 5 to 7 percent even during the Civil War, why, historians asks, did the government charge the railroads 6 percent on loans that would not finance more than one-third of the construction costs? They further contend that the government's shortsighted policy encouraged Dr. Durant to set up the Credit Mobilier, which in turn led to the Ames-Durant, Dodge-Durant, and Dodge-Seymour feuds during the building of the Union Pacific. It also led to the charge in Congress that UP officials used Credit Mobilier stock to bribe congressmen and other government officials in order to obtain favorable treatment.

The scapegoat of the Credit Mobilier scandal was Oakes Ames, who was a member of the House of Representatives as well as vice-president of the UP and a director of Credit Mobilier. Ames admitted that he had sold Credit Mobilier stock to public officials without requiring them to make down payments. Among those receiving stock were Schuyler Colfax, Speaker of the House and President Grant's vice-president in 1868–72, and James A. Garfield, a member of the House. Colfax's political career was wrecked, but Garfield was elected President of the United States in 1880. The House refused to expel Ames, but it publicly censured him in 1873. He died of a heart attack a few weeks later.

The Big Four of the Central Pacific — Stanford, Huntington, Hopkins, and Crocker — quickly realized that their hope for profit lay in developing a railroad and steamship empire that would give them control of the West Coast traffic from Oregon

A handbill announcing the grand opening of service on the newly-laid railroad from the Atlantic to the Pacific.

to Mexico as well as east to Utah and Louisiana. Thus they made the Southern Pacific Company, which they had chartered in California in 1865, a prosperous business by building a number of small railroads in southern California in the 1870's, and buying several Texas railroads in the early 1880's. Then, in 1884, the Southern Pacific and Central Pacific were combined.

The tracks of the Union Pacific had built up Nebraska and Wyoming as grain and cattle states, and they could have tapped the resources and business of Colorado, Utah, Idaho, Oregon, Arizona, and even California. However, the UP's failure to build a transportation empire matching that of the Southern Pacific could be traced to Dr. Durant's urge to "grab a wad" of money and get out. Badly managed by shortsighted men, the Union Pacific eventually went into bankruptcy during the Panic of 1893. But under the management of Edward H. Harriman, who reorganized the road in 1897–98, the Union Pacific became an important and prosperous company. Despite its ups and downs, the Union Pacific remained a monument to the engineering genius of Grenville Mellen Dodge. The care with which Dodge had directed the surveys of the UP was demonstrated when Harriman took over the road. Although Harriman spent millions of dollars rebuilding and straightening the line, the distance from Omaha to Ogden was only cut by less than 40 miles.

One hundred years after the famous link-up, on May 10, 1969, a troupe of collegiate actors, local residents, and servicemen reenacted the driving of the Last Spike, now called the Golden Spike, at Promontory, Utah. And the National Park Service dedicated a visitors' center and museum at Golden Spike National Historic Site. Its attractions now include a mile of restored track and two old-fashioned locomotives. Today, the spot where the UP and CP engines touched cowcatchers lies 30 miles from the present transcontinental railroad route across Great Salt Lake.

Silent and lonely, 80 miles north of Salt Lake City, Promontory long was neglected by tourists, but now the Golden Spike National Historic Site is expected to attract a growing number of visitors each year.

Bibliography

Griswold, Wesley S. *A Work of Giants*. New York: McGraw-Hill Book Company, 1962.

Holbrook, Stewart. *The Story of American Railroads*. New York: Crown Publishers, 1947.

Howard, Robert W. *The Great Iron Trail*. New York: Bonanza Books, 1962.

Kraus, George. *High Road to Promontory*. Palo Alto: American West Publishing Company, 1969.

Sabin, Edwin. *Building the Pacific Railway*. Philadelphia: J. B. Lippincott, 1919.

Index